IN MY OWN WORDS

IN MY OWN WORDS

EVITA

TRANSLATED FROM THE SPANISH
BY LAURA DAIL

THE NEW PRESS · NEW YORK

All photographs were provided by the National Archive of Argentina.
We are grateful for its permission to reprint them.

LIBRARY OF CONGRESS CATALOG CARD NUMBER
96-69626

ISBN
1-56584-353-3

Published in the United States by The New Press, New York
Distributed by W. W. Norton & Company, Inc., New York

*Established in 1990 as a major alternative to the large commercial publishing
houses, The New Press is a nonprofit book
publisher. The Press is operated editorially
in the public interest, rather than for
private gain; it is committed to publishing,*
*in innovative ways, works of educational,
cultural, and community value that,
despite their intellectual merits, might not
normally be commercially viable. The
New Press's editorial offices are located
at the City University of New York.*

Book design by Smyth, Smith, and Whiteside of BAD
Production management by Kim Waymer
Printed in the United States of America

9 8 7 6 5 4 3 2 1

CONTENTS

INTRODUCTION

BY JOSEPH A. PAGE*

THE DISCOVERY OF A DOCUMENT PROBABLY BASED IN PART ON dictation by the wife of Argentine President Juan Perón just before she died in 1952, but recently denounced as a hoax and forgery by her surviving sisters, provides further evidence of how difficult it is to locate the real person behind the myths shrouding the figure the world knows simply as Evita.[1]

Mi mensaje, or "My Message," presents itself as the death-bed testimonial of Eva Perón. In the final stages of her unsuccessful struggle against the ravages of uterine cancer, the First Lady told visitors that she was working on a text that would convey her farewell message to the people of Argentina. But in the immediate aftermath of her death, the book remained unpublished.

Although immediately following her death several public references were made to the existence of a manuscript written by Evita, the text of what purports to be her parting words was not published until 1987. Thus, the manuscript did not reach Evita's intended audience during either the remainder of Perón's presidency, which ended in a 1955 military coup, or Perón's brief return to power in the 1970s.

What was heralded as the long-lost document finally came to light in 1987, when Peronist historian Fermín Chávez published *Mi mensaje.* The emotional, at times bitter, tract extolled the virtue of fanaticism as the only acceptable mind-set for the Peronist faithful, and it attacked unnamed members of the military and the Roman Catholic clergy for plotting against her husband.

* Joseph A. Page, a professor at the Georgetown University Law Center, is the author of *Perón: A Biography,* the Spanish translation of which made the best-seller list in Argentina for five months. His most recent book, *The Brazilians,* has been published in Argentina under the title *Brasil.*

In his introduction to the book Chávez presents evidence that the text was the work of Eva Perón. A second edition, published by Futuro in 1994, contains statements by others supporting Chávez's position, and the testimony of one of Evita's former secretaries, asserting that he was the person who took down her dictation. Tomás Eloy Martínez, a journalist whose novel *Santa Evita* was a best-seller in Argentina, also holds that "Mi mensaje" is most probably the work of Eva Perón.

Yet there is reason to react with caution to these claims. Ghostwriters were responsible for what purports to be her autobiography as well as another book published under her name. Speechwriters drafted her public addresses (and her husband edited them). The contents of *Mi mensaje* easily lend themselves to political and hagiographical uses by people with agendas of their own. The "last wishes" set out in a letter hand-written by Evita to her husband shortly before her death are quite different from those expressed in the "Supreme Will" read aloud by Perón from the balcony of the Government House on October 17, 1952 (and included as a chapter in *Mi mensaje*). According to Eva Perón's biographers Nicolas Fraser and Marysa Navarro, these "'last wishes'…could be those of another person." Moreover, the two surviving sisters of Evita, who control her estate, maintain that she neither wrote nor dictated what appears in the book.

Why is it important whether "My Message" conveys the actual words or thoughts of Eva Perón? After all, figures from the political, entertainment, and sports worlds have long utilized the literary talents of others to present to the reading public authorized versions of their ideas and of themselves. If the book is a complete fabrication, it would of course greatly matter, but as this introduction will demonstrate, the text reflects much of the real Eva Perón. How much, is a question about which reasonable minds may differ. Evita has often taken on the form of an illusion, reflecting the preconceptions and fantasies of the viewer, and anything that sheds light on who she really was is welcome.

Misgivings about the genuineness of "My Message" illustrate how difficult it is to get a handle on the real Eva Perón. Among her fellow Argentines and foreigners alike, she has provoked love and hatred, admiration and contempt, fascination and indifference, and last but not least, a thick cloud of bewilderment. Her capacity to stir these responses is central to the mystique that continues to surround her.

The search for the historical Eva Perón must rely on a limited collection of primary and secondary sources: photographs and documentary film footage; one motion picture in its entirety and portions of another; texts and audio tapes of her speeches; a few letters written in her own hand; several books in her name; and a plethora of published and recorded testimonials by, or second-hand accounts attributed to, individuals who had, or claim that they had, personal contact with her. To complicate matters, new material relating to her keeps surfacing.

In addition, there are the various myths that have attached to her. They are as much a part of Eva Perón as the jewelry and furs she liked to wear, and they tell us how people saw, and continue to see, her. They also affect the credibility of those who have provided raw material for her biographers.

The text of "My Message" has to be read in the context of the facts we know about Evita's life as well as the legends that have blossomed around her. The story of her life, and the mythology surrounding it, shed light both on the book and on the arguments for and against its genuineness. The document, in turn, illuminates both the real and the legendary Eva Perón.

During the seven scant years she held center stage in her native land, Eva María Duarte de Perón was called the second most powerful person in Argentina and the most powerful woman on the planet. To atone for these and other sins, she has been made the subject of a mercifully short-running Broadway play (*The Diamond Orchid*), a soft-porn movie (*Little Mother*), a satirical farce in Paris (*Eva Perón*, starring a female impersonator), a boring TV mini-series (starring Faye Dunaway), and the powerful but historically inaccurate rock opera *Evita*.

The global popularity of the latter, and the widespread interest in the motion picture based on it, attest to the enduring mystique of Eva Perón. Her meteoric life, premature death, and the bizarre postmortem odyssey of her embalmed corpse are the stuff of fiction. But who was the real Eva Perón?

Eva María Ibarguren came into the world on May 7, 1919, in a small town in the province of Buenos Aires. She was the youngest of five children born to a married rancher named Juan Duarte and one of his employees, Juana Ibarguren, whom he kept as his mistress. The mores of the time did not prevent him from maintaining two families, as long as his concubine and her brood remained out of view. Juana, on the other hand, did not hesitate to adopt for her offspring the surname Duarte.

When Juan Duarte died in an auto accident in 1926, his legal wife refused to allow Eva, her mother, or her siblings to enter the mortuary where his remains lay, and forced them to stay outside, peering in, until one of Duarte's relatives took pity on them and let them make a quick pass by the flower-bedecked cadaver. He also allowed them to follow the tail end of the funeral procession, but only as far as the cemetery gate.

This bitter experience would fester in Eva's memory for the rest of her life. She would never truly shed the stigma of illegitimacy, either in her own mind or in the eyes of those who invoked Argentina's strict social codes and conservative Catholicism as justifications for their rejection of her.[2]

The young Eva was forced to endure the social ostracism that attached to her illegitimacy, which at that point in time in Argentina carried the weight of a curse. Since the circumstances of her birth had been completely beyond her control, the injustice of the opprobrium directed at her must surely have rankled her. She sought refuge by fantasizing about the lives of show business celebrities chronicled in fan magazines.

Although she completed six grades of primary school, formal education did not particularly interest her. As she entered her teens she was an attractive youngster, slender and brunette, with pale skin and large brown eyes. She liked to sing but was not vocally gifted. Her stage debut in a school play in 1933 may not have electrified the audience, but it convinced Eva that she had seen a glimpse of the future.

Her three older sisters pointed the way to respectability by marrying into the middle class. Evita, however, decided to seek her fortune in Buenos Aires. According to one account, she attached herself to a popular tango singer who was touring the provinces, and traveled with him and his wife to the capital. A derogatory version, often repeated by her enemies and embraced by the rock opera *Evita*, has her seducing the singer in order to escape her hometown.

This was the starting point for the myth of "Evita the Whore." According to rabid Evita-haters, she worked as a prostitute to support herself during her years as a struggling actress in Argentina's "Big Apple." One of her detractors was the renowned Argentine author Jorge Luis Borges, who suffered a number of indignities at the hands of the Peronists. As late as 1980 he was calling her a "common prostitute," and was repeating the anti-Peronist joke that circulated when the legislature of the province of Buenos Aires debated whether to change the name of the city of La Plata to Eva Perón: "Why so much discussion between La Plata and Eva Perón? Why don't they call it 'La Pluta'?" (a play on words combining La Plata and *puta*, the Spanish word for prostitute).[3] All reliable accounts of Evita's life reject this charge as totally groundless.

These were the testing years of her life. She survived on grit and with the help of friends. Within months of her arrival in Buenos Aires she had secured a bit part in a play. Soon she won several more minor roles and had her photo published in a magazine. In 1937 she appeared in her first motion picture and her first radio drama. The parts she played were still secondary, but they were becoming more frequent and more substantial. Fan-magazine exposure also increased.

Evita's detractors have insisted that during this period she engaged in a series of meretricious relationships with men who she thought might advance her career. The rock opera libretto depicts a hard-as-nails Evita, whirling through revolving doors from bedroom to bedroom, seducing lovers who might help her and then discarding them when they outlived their usefulness.

The Fraser-Navarro biography, based on extensive interviews and documentation, convincingly puts to rest this canard. Indeed, it is equally plausible to speculate that casting directors and others forced the teenager to submit to their advances. The common practice of fan magazines to invent romances for the starlets they publicized, as well as the low esteem in which polite Argentine society held theatrical people, fortified the myth that Evita led a sexually active life during this period.

Eva the aspiring actress was insecure, ambitious, and restless. Rough edges still marked her speech and behavior, and her colleagues made fun of her lack of acting talent, lack of vocabulary, and poor diction. Her pushiness occasionally produced excesses, such as occurred when she pestered Carmen Miranda and wouldn't leave her apartment during one of the Brazilian singer's tours of Argentina.[4]

In 1939 Evita obtained a co-starring role in a radio melodrama. As the Fraser-Navarro biography puts it, "Evita was good at conveying suffering. When she found the soaps she found her acting career." Radio theater in Latin America utilized a distinctive, overheated prose that would leave its mark on Evita. Many of her addresses as First Lady would incorporate melodramatic rhetoric (indeed, an author of radio dramas served for years as one of her speechwriters), and her own style of speaking and writing borrowed heavily from the genre.

These were the days when she sat for the photos that would supply the grist for a later campaign to discredit her. A 1940 movie magazine published them under the heading "Eva Duarte Surprised by the Camera." They displayed the winsome brunette in various pinup poses that bared her legs, shoulders, and a bit of breast. By the norms of the day the pictures might have been daring, but they did not go beyond existing limits. Her enemies, however, would later reproduce and distribute them as "skin pics," behavior that offers a glimpse into the salacious side of the hostility she generated.

By 1943 Eva was starring in a radio series called *Heroines of History*. She played such figures as the Empress Josephine of France, Tsarina Alexandra and Catherine the Great of Russia, Elizabeth I of England, Madame Chiang Kai-shek, Lady Emma Hamilton (the mistress of Lord Horatio Nelson), Sarah Bernhardt, and Isadora Duncan. Life would soon imitate art.

On June 4, 1943, the Argentine military overthrew the government, and Army officers assumed power. At a benefit for victims of an earthquake in western Argentina Eva met a dashing colonel who had been placed in charge of the regime's relations with the nation's labor unions and had emerged as the strong man behind the generals ostensibly running the country. There was an immediate chemistry between them, and soon the 24-year-old actress and the 49-year-old widower were living together. For the next eight years Eva Duarte and Juan Perón would be inseparable.

Perón, like Eva, had been born out of wedlock, and he shared with her a contempt for "respectable" Argentines. Before he met Eva, he'd not only lived with a teenage girl (whom he nicknamed "Piranha" because of her bite), but had flaunted her as his "daughter." Cohabiting with Eva was another way for him to thumb his nose at society.

Evita was open, uninhibited, and outspoken, qualities that he liked. Instead of fading into the woodwork when the colonel invited military, political, and trade-union associates to their apartment, she sat in on their meetings and did not hesitate to offer opinions.

Evita used her relationship with Perón to further her career. She began to exert influence over the Government Press Office, which had considerable control over Argentina's entertainment industry. In addition, she was given her best role yet in a movie called *La cabalgata del circo* (*Circus Cavalcade*), notable only because it required her to bleach her hair, and she remained a blonde for the rest of her life. During the filming Evita was rumored to have quarreled with and received a slap in the face from Libertad Lamarque, a well-known star whose subsequent disappearance from Argentine movies was attributed to Evita's custom of punishing her enemies (and who, in an autobiography published in 1986, denied that the incident ever occurred).[5]

There were all kinds of whispers about the money Evita was now making, but they are impossible to confirm. Given the way businesses traditionally dealt with government regulation in Argentina and in light of Evita's financially insecure background, it would not be unreasonable to assume that she extracted some pecuniary reward in exchange for the benefit of her growing influence over the federal bureaucracy.

Her association with Perón at this time also fueled charges that became the basis for another of the myths: "Evita the Nazi." Evita was accused of being a Nazi agent who earned a fortune from the sale of passports to Nazis escaping from the beleaguered Third Reich in the waning months of World War II. A stream of German submarines was supposed to have carried gold and other valuables to Argentina, in return for documents that could be used by fleeing Nazi officials. This treasure was said to have ended up in bank accounts belonging to Evita, who was charged with playing an active role in all these machinations.

The original source of this myth was a book written by an anti-Peronist politician and supposedly based on German documents discovered immediately after the war. Other writers revived the allegation in the 1970s.

The basis for the myth is clearly false. Proof of Evita's involvement rests upon letters written by a German naval captain and dated 1941 and 1943. They refer to Perón's liaison with the actress, a relationship that did not begin until January of 1944. They also locate Perón at a poker game in the German embassy in Buenos Aires at a time when he was actually in Europe.

A box of documents stored in the National Archives in Washington and containing material about German submarines that did reach Argentina fails to confirm in any way that a Nazi treasure had been smuggled into the country. Indeed, there is evidence that stories of high Nazi officials converting their property into gold and fleeing Europe by submarine originated in a British "black propaganda" operation designed to persuade German soldiers and civilians that their leaders were deserting them.

To a certain degree, the Nazi-Fascist taint applied to Evita amounts to guilt by association, inasmuch as it was her paramour who said and did things that suggested sympathy for the Axis. Juan Perón had served as an Argentine military attaché in Italy just before the war, freely borrowed political ideas from Italian fascism, openly admired Mussolini and the efficiency of the German army, and had close friends within Argentina's German community.

Eva's sudden notoriety disgusted many high-ranking military officials. Her behavior, often crude and overbearing, and the suspicion that she was personally profiting from the influence she now exerted outraged members of the officer corps, some of whom had other reasons to be displeased with Perón. The appointment of one of her friends to a high position within the regime was the last straw; the Army forced Perón's resignation from his government post and put him under arrest.

On October 17, 1945, a day that would change the course of Argentine history, a large crowd of workers converged in front of the Government House in Buenos Aires to demand Perón's release. The colonel had intervened in labor disputes on the side of the unions, secured the passage of laws granting benefits to workers, and had changed the government's attitude toward labor by treating the unions with respect rather than repressing them. Now his cultivation of the workers paid off handsomely, as the *descamisados*, or "shirtless ones" as they would be called in the Peronist lexicon, took control of the streets. The demonstration forced the regime to bring Perón back and let him address the crowd from the balcony. Elections were then scheduled, and the colonel entered the lists as a candidate.

The incident on October 17 spawned yet another myth, that of "Evita the Power Behind Perón."[6] It was Evita, according to legend, who personally mobilized the *descamisados* and sent them marching into downtown Buenos Aires. (The most far-fetched version, published in an American magazine in 1952, had Evita dragging her lover into the Government House and pushing him out onto the balcony.) Perón's enemies used the myth to denigrate him by suggesting he was a sniveling coward who had to be rescued from the jaws of oblivion by a woman. The rock opera *Evita* perpetuates the myth by depicting its title character as a power-hungry vixen who drove her paramour to seek political control of Argentina.

Interestingly, faithful Peronists accept the same version of Eva's participation in the events of October 17, but for different reasons. For them, Eva's supposed role in securing her colonel's release was proof of unswerving devotion both to Perón and to Argentina's working class.

In fact, Evita had nothing to do with what happened on October 17. Labor leaders whom Perón had courted spread the word of his arrest, and the rank and file, concerned about what had happened to the man who had come to symbolize their aspirations, willingly and eagerly converged on the Government House.

Shortly after Perón's dramatic release, he and Eva legalized their relationship in both a civil and religious wedding ceremony. The marriage certificate stated that the bride's name was Eva Duarte and subtracted several years from her age. Her actual birth certificate, which listed her name as Eva María Ibarguren and recorded her correct date of birth, was then destroyed.

Evita played a limited role during the presidential campaign. She accompanied Perón on several trips to the interior, yet remained discreetly in the background. This did not prevent her from becoming a target of smear campaigns based upon the myth of "Evita the Nazi" and launched by the North American press against her. An article in *Life* magazine stated that "Evita occupies much the same position in the Perón machine that Goering's actress wife did in Nazi Germany."

On February 22, 1946, after what was generally recognized as the cleanest campaign in Argentine history, Juan Perón was elected president. He took the oath of office on June 4, and set in motion what would soon be known as the Perón era.

Eva's contribution to this era had been eerily foreshadowed in the last film she made. Early in 1945 she used her influence to secure the title role in a film called *La pródiga* (*The Generous Woman*). Its scriptwriter demonstrated a considerable ineptness at developing characters and plot, but he did display an uncanny power of prophesy. He had peasants call Evita's character the "Mother of the Poor" and the "Sister of the Sad" (they also constantly refer to her as "*La Señora*," or "The Lady"), and the title character is a kind of "Lady Bountiful," always doing things for the less fortunate.[7] In the course of the next several years, Eva Perón would create her own real-life version of *La pródiga*.

When the young, street-smart, totally instinctive Evita became her country's First Lady, she brought to the role a disarming, often ingenuous freshness and a style that some would find tasteless. At one of the inaugural banquets she wore a gray silk gown that left one of her shoulders bare. Protocol required her to sit next to the cardinal of Buenos Aires. Photos that appeared in the press captured the event for posterity and scandalized upper-class Argentines.

One of the first things she did as First Lady was to find good government jobs for members of her family. This set her apart from her husband, whose only concession to the tradition of nepotism was to install his older brother as head zookeeper of Buenos Aires.

From the very beginning it was clear that Evita would participate in more than just ceremonial activities. Even before the inauguration, she had given a speech thanking Argentine women (who did not have the right to vote) for their organizational support of her husband and urging Congress to enfranchise them. Soon after Perón's inauguration she moved into her own office and began involving herself in various minor governmental matters. The president did nothing to discourage his wife. He had no interest in day-to-day administration, and was happy to give Evita a free rein in such matters. His minister of labor, whose meekness apparently got him the job, became her virtual errand boy.

The First Lady had no political views of her own, and quickly absorbed those of her husband, whose ideas she never questioned. But she had no qualms about making her views known on mundane managerial matters, which generally resolved themselves according to her dictates. On this level she relied on intuition and energy, qualities she possessed in abundance. Loyalty was the virtue she prized most highly when she made personnel decisions. This invited exploitation, especially by opportunists who had little else to offer except lapdog fidelity.

Soon she was representing her husband at ceremonial functions, where she read texts that speechwriters prepared for her. Her voice was shrill, her delivery stilted, but she was gaining valuable experience in the art of platform oratory. She liked to present herself as "Comrade Evita," the girl from the provinces, and struck a chord with lower-class listeners, who responded to her with enthusiasm.

The role into which she was moving was that of Perón's surrogate contact with the common people of Argentina. In the beginning, her performances lacked polish, as she struggled to master the subtleties of her new position. When she spoke off the cuff, what she said and how she said it came from the heart and bore unmistakable traces of her disadvantaged past.

She developed a childlike ostentation in dress and accessories. Her fixation on jewelry invited those who sought favors to ply her with precious gems. It was a weakness that easily lent itself to abuse.

If Evita's ambitions had been merely to please her husband and ingratiate herself with his Peronist followers, she would have achieved them without question. But she also sought social acceptance, and benign tolerance had never been a virtue of the Argentine elite. They refused to welcome a First Lady who had dubious origins and was an ex-actress. The Charitable Society, a foundation created and run by the patrician families of Buenos Aires, had by custom given first ladies the title of honorary president, but they refused to bestow this honor on Eva Perón, because of her "youth," they said. Evita's classic rejoinder was: "If they can't accept me, let them name my mother."

Then came a momentous opportunity for her. *Generalísimo* Francisco Franco invited her to visit Spain, and similar bids came from the Italian and French governments. Since trips to Europe had long been an indispensable part of the upper-class curriculum vitae, Evita saw this as a way to demonstrate that she too could tour the Continent in style.

While resentment may partially explain Eva's eagerness to travel abroad, her self-image as an embryonic historical personage should not be overlooked. She once admitted to a friend that she wanted to "cut a figure in history." As a radio performer she had played a number of great women. Now, in her own eyes, she would join their ranks. The European tour would thrust her into a global spotlight and help her find a niche in history books, social acceptance or rejection by the Argentine oligarchy notwithstanding.

However, the thought of leaving both husband and homeland raised all kinds of anxieties in Evita. On the eve of her departure she wrote Perón a letter in which her fears tumbled out in a torrent of emotional words that were earthy and at times ungrammatical.[8] The document is genuine (photocopies of this and other letters Evita wrote have been published in *El último Perón*, by Esteban Peicovich). It provides a rare glimpse into the heart and mind of the real Eva Perón, expressing her sorrow at leaving her husband, her great love for him, and her struggles to convey her feelings adequately. She included instructions to be followed in the event of her death, and urged him not to believe rumors, which she did not specify, about her childhood.

What came to be known as the "Rainbow Tour" was on the whole a success, as the glamorous Evita provided postwar Europe with what the rock opera calls a "little touch of/Argentina's brand of/Star quality." She was hailed by large crowds in Spain, and the U.S. ambassador to that country begrudgingly summed up the visit as "something of a triumph." He added that "she carried out a difficult task with poise and intelligence."[9] Evita also beguiled the French, and enjoyed a private audience with Pope Pius XII.

There were relatively few bumpy moments. Demonstrators in Italy made uncomplimentary references to the ideological kinship between her husband and Mussolini. A visit to England never materialized because the Royal Family made it clear that they would not receive her, and she refused to accept anything that even hinted of a snub.

The "Evita the Nazi" myth resurfaced during the trip. The international press reported that she returned Fascist salutes while crowds hailed her in Spain. Newsreel footage shows her gesturing in a way that detractors might maliciously have interpreted as the open-handed Fascist greeting, but as the Fraser-Navarro biography points out, it was "only her habitual gesture of putting her hand high above her head and waving it." As a result of her brief visit to Switzerland, the rumor mill alleged that she deposited in numbered bank accounts the vast fortune she had acquired from the sale of passports to fleeing officials of the Third Reich. However, the decision to go to Switzerland was not made until Evita was already in Paris, which undercuts the suggestion that she had planned to engage in financial transactions during the trip.

The "Rainbow Tour" established Evita as a political figure in her own right. The trip generated considerable publicity abroad, and even though much of it was sensationalistic, trivial, or negative, the fact that she had kept Argentina in the international spotlight was a signal accomplishment in a country that has always had a fixation with how the rest of the world sees it.

Shortly after her return, Evita made public appearances promoting legislation that would extend to Argentine women the right to vote, and Congress quickly gave its approval. Perón signed the bill into law and presented it to his wife as the representative of those whom it enfranchised.

The First Lady also thrust herself into activities affecting both the labor movement and social welfare. In March 1948 she intervened in a work dispute involving bank employees and helped to settle it. Shortly thereafter the government approved a corporate entity known as the María Eva Duarte de Perón Social Aid Foundation (later to be retitled the Eva Perón Foundation), which became the vehicle for her efforts on behalf of the less fortunate.

At the same time, Evita took good care of the members of her immediate family. Her brother had already been installed as the president's private secretary. One brother-in-law was appointed to the Supreme Court of Argentina, another became a senator from the province of Buenos Aires, and a third took over as director of customs for the port of Buenos Aires. Two of her sisters obtained government jobs.

The relationship between Juan and Eva Perón formed the bedrock upon which rested Evita's reputation as the most powerful woman in the contemporary world. The president trusted her. He was very cynical about human nature and felt uncomfortable toward any Peronist who demonstrated genuine leadership capabilities. But Evita was a different story. Her influence derived totally from him, to such an extent that she could never threaten his authority or compete with him. He might have oversimplified when he was quoted as saying that Eva Perón was "a product of mine," but it was this feeling that let him view with equanimity the political heights she was beginning to scale.

Evita accepted without hesitation the role Perón fashioned for her. She never tired of heaping extravagant praise upon him. No doubt this reflected her own insecurity. What made her comfortable in her new position as political First Lady was that it permitted her to pursue her relentless "ambition to be someone."

In many ways Perón and Evita complemented each other. Their disparate traits meshed together nicely to make them a formidable team. Perón was the grand master of the subtle maneuver, while Evita acted out of impulse. Perón liked to play the statesman. Evita relished lashing out at the oligarchy and other enemies, real and imagined. (In this way, they performed a kind of "good-cop-bad-cop" routine.) Responsibility was something Perón shied away from, especially in matters such as the replacement of important members of his inner circle. Evita's passionate likes and dislikes furnished both a sword for his political executions and a shield behind which he could take refuge.

Perón abhorred spontaneous physical contact. He was superb at haranguing crowds from a balcony, but refused to mingle with them and expose himself to adulation at close range. Evita, however, mingled easily and willingly with her public. When she held open house in her office for anyone who wanted to bring problems to her, she customarily kissed women visitors as they departed. Once, a poet who was attending one of these sessions attempted to throw himself between the First Lady and a supplicant with a syphilitic sore on her mouth. Evita brushed the poet away and pressed her lips against the cheek of the unfortunate woman. "Never do that again," she warned him later. "It's the price I have to pay."

Having fought her way up from poverty, Evita could symbolize the Argentine working class and the dispossessed. Perón let her grow into this role, whereby she became a tribune for the *descamisados*, whom she represented before her husband and whose needs she articulated. Proximity to the president made her the perfect intermediary, from the points of view of both those she represented and of Perón, who could now control the demands of his followers.

For Perón, the ideals he espoused were tactics, disposable or adaptable as circumstances dictated. His wife, a professional actress accustomed to playing parts, came to believe the words put into her mouth. She *became* Evita with an ardor that made her more Peronist than Perón himself.

The fact that the couple never produced any children[10] inevitably provoked whispers. According to one speculative hypothesis, their union was not based upon a sexual relationship, but rather upon the fusion of two wills, both fueled by a burning passion for power; Evita saw in Perón the father she had never had, and the commanding figure who could satisfy her ambitions; Perón saw in Evita someone he could use for political purposes; though passionate, the hypothesis goes, Evita was indifferent toward sex; Perón was both cold and sexually indifferent.

In any case, the hours they kept would not seem to have permitted much intimacy. Perón, a career military man, liked to rise and go to bed early. Evita rose late, worked feverishly all day and into the evening at her social welfare activities.

Speculation about Perón's relationships with women could not help but rub off on Evita. He had a very cold attitude toward his mother, with whom he maintained virtually no contact. He also had a predilection for very young girls, as evidenced by his dalliance with "Piranha" and, subsequent to Evita's death, the scandals surrounding the attention he showered on high-school teenagers (one became his mistress).

As a young Army officer, he had married an attractive 17-year-old blonde named Aurelia Tizón, and by all accounts the couple enjoyed a happy life together (until her untimely death from uterine cancer in 1938), except for their failure to produce a child. According to one account, Aurelia had a medical examination that concluded the problem was not hers.[11] An alternative explanation for Perón's supposed sterility was that it resulted from an injury to his spermatic cords sustained during a motorcycle accident in Italy.

In 1993 the accepted belief in Perón's infertility was shaken by a declaration attributed to his third wife, Isabel, that she had become pregnant by him in 1957 and 1958, but both pregnancies had ended in miscarriages. Even more interesting was an unconfirmed report that surfaced at the same time to the effect that Evita had suffered a miscarriage in 1945.[12]

Perón's relationship with his second wife reinforced the myth of "Evita the Power Behind Perón." According to this interpretation, Evita was the dominant partner, the real macho who exercised de facto control over Argentina. All historical evidence suggests quite the reverse.

On the other hand, it would be equally erroneous to regard Evita as no more than Perón's mindless instrument. Perón did nudge his wife into her political role, yet she was predisposed to accept it, and she carried it off with great gusto. He did manipulate her and benefit from the way she promoted him. However, it was always in her interest to aggrandize him. She in turn accumulated political muscle and did not hesitate to use it, often capriciously. But in every instance it was authority that he delegated to her or that he did not wish to wield.

This interpretation does not denigrate Evita. Given the enormous political imbalance that had previously existed between the genders in Argentina, the power that she was able to exercise and the way she encouraged female involvement in political activity represented a quantum leap forward for Argentine women.

Totally committed to Perón, Evita exuded a zealousness and enthusiasm that lent a distinctive touch to the movement that bore her husband's name. She was the emotional center of Peronism, and provided it with a heart and soul. Yet there were times when the lack of formal limits on her activities and the fervor that defined her would create problems for the president. The very qualities that were the essence of Evita carried with them the potential for excess that could embarrass Perón.

By 1950 Eva Perón had consolidated her various roles and was charging ahead with all the energy she could muster. She was involving herself actively in both personnel and trade union matters. She also stood at the forefront of the women's branch of the Peronist movement, a constituency that was becoming increasingly significant as a political force. But her hand was most visible on the social welfare front.

The María Eva Duarte de Perón Social Aid Foundation had by now grown into a gigantic enterprise dominating virtually all public as well as private charitable activity and extending into the fields of education and health. At first it ran on voluntary contributions from individuals and groups eager to gain Eva's good graces. Then the national trade union federation voted to give the Foundation two days' pay per year from every worker's salary, and every worker's annual salary increase for one month. A government decree put into the Foundation's coffers 20 percent of the annual income from the national lottery.

The Foundation's actual record was impressive. It built homes for orphans, unwed mothers, and the elderly; shelters for working women; lunch facilities for children; children's hospitals; vacation colonies for workers; low-cost housing; and schools for nurses. On several highly publicized occasions it dispatched foreign aid, such as provisions for Ecuadorian earthquake victims, toys for Italian children, and even clothing for needy children in Washington.

In public utterances Eva Perón maintained that the Foundation's goal was not to promote philanthropy, but rather to achieve social justice, which was one of the stated goals of Peronism. She declared that she was merely returning to the poor what had been unfairly taken away from them. But she never explained why the Peronist government did not attempt to use the powers at its disposal to eliminate the causes of social and economic injustice, rather than dispense palliatives.

What lent the Foundation its unique character was the way it was totally identified with the figure of Eva Perón. The cult of personality had by now taken hold in Argentina. Perón was the maximum leader—the "Great Conductor," as he was often called—and Evita, through the Foundation, became the nation's "Lady Bountiful."

Visitors marveled at the way she held court in her office, where poor people would line up to see her and she would attend to every one of them. An article published in the *New York Times Magazine* in 1948 described how she would hand out money and medicines (generally streptomycin). When the reporter asked her in writing whether she kept any financial accounts, she replied in the negative, adding that "none will be," because the Foundation was not a "business proposition." This *modus operandi* encouraged rumors that Evita and her inner circle were siphoning off funds from the Foundation, a charge that has never been proved.

The force field of emotion that generated Evita's social welfare activities in turn bestirred strong passions in those who benefited from them. One product of this reciprocity was the emergence of the myth of "Evita the Good," and even "Saint Evita." The Peronist-controlled press lavished upon her titles such as the "Lady of Hope" and the "Spiritual Mother of All Argentines," and society's underlings readily accepted the legitimacy of these epithets.

In many ways Perón and Evita were at the pinnacle in 1950. Effective political opposition to them no longer existed. Organized labor had been virtually incorporated into the government. The mass media, now under total Peronist control, sang their praises in unison. People now customarily referred to the president's wife as "*La Señora*," or "The Lady." Her faithful followers used the term with reverence, her enemies with unconcealed sarcasm.

But 1950 was also the year when Evita's health problems surfaced and cast a dark cloud over her future. In January she complained of inguinal pain, and her physician diagnosed her condition as acute appendicitis. He later claimed that while she was hospitalized, she underwent tests that indicated she was suffering from uterine cancer. He advised her to have a hysterectomy, but Evita refused, angrily maintaining that the diagnosis served the interests of her enemies, who wanted to remove her from the political scene.

The First Lady had suffered chronic health problems throughout her adult life. She had occasionally succumbed to sickness or exhaustion, but refused to slow down because, as she once told a U.S. diplomat, the *descamisados* needed her. In addition, there is evidence that she was suffering from an anemic condition, and that she was taking blood transfusions.

Evita's doctor later insisted that if she had submitted to a hysterectomy when her cancer was discovered, she might well have avoided the agony that would follow. He pointed out that her mother had had a similar cancer, but after a hysterectomy she lived to a ripe old age.

Why did Evita refuse surgery? She may not have fully undertood what was wrong with her. If she did, one plausible interpretation of her behavior is that she could not bring herself to allow the removal of her womb. Psychological and perhaps even cultural pressures may have made it impossible for the "Spiritual Mother of All Argentine Children" to cope with the symbolism of a hysterectomy. Rather than face the crisis rationally, she may have embraced the paranoid suspicion that the diagnosis was somehow the work of enemies who wanted not just to force her into a prolonged convalescence, but also to destroy her last physical link to motherhood.

Despite the deterioration of her health, the First Lady refused to slow down, thus fortifying the myth of "Evita the Good." Indeed, Peronists would later maintain as an article of faith that her love for the poor caused her to sacrifice her energy, her health, and ultimately her life in a form of martyrdom.

While the cancer gnawed away at her, she was reaching her apogee as a political figure. Evita was the force that galvanized the entire Peronist movement, from Perón and his acolytes to the lowliest of the poor. She supplied the magnetic current that linked the leader to his followers. She also complemented him exquisitely, her violent rhetoric enabling him to play the unifier, her contact with people freeing him for more elevated matters of state, her manipulation of the bureaucracy shielding him from the unpleasantness of imposing discipline. In carrying out his directions, responding to his subtle hints, and exercising her own discretion, she served his needs perfectly.

But the moment was now approaching when she would be tempted to go beyond the bounds he placed upon her political role. She would be as unsuccessful at achieving this as she would be in resisting the disease that was silently devouring her from within.

Presidential elections were scheduled for November of 1951, and there could be no doubt that Perón would win a second term. The political opposition had by now succumbed to repressive measures adopted by the Peronists and its own ineptness. But the vice presidential slot offered temptations to the ambitious, since it was currently held by an aged politician who was no more than a figurehead.

Both the labor unions and the women's movement saw advantages to be gained by pushing Evita's candidacy. Perón liked to force the various elements of the Peronist movement to compete with one another for his favor. It was a way he could control them. With Evita as vice president, representing their interests, labor leaders and Peronist women felt that they could escape the adversary roles Perón had assigned to them.

Moreover, Evita herself seems not only to have done nothing to stop the push for her candidacy, but also actively to have encouraged it. Perhaps she saw this as the crowning achievement in her lifelong effort to "be someone." Or perhaps this represented an effort on her part to sublimate her awareness that she had cancer.

During the first half of 1951, momentum mounted for a Perón-Perón ticket. The president did not commit himself, but instead let things take their course. The national trade union confederation scheduled an "open meeting" on August 22, when they planned to offer Evita the vice presidential nomination.

But the military could not stomach the possibility that a woman —especially *that* woman—might become their commander in chief. Army officers were now actively conspiring against Perón, although they lacked organization and widespread support even within the Armed Forces. An Evita candidacy, however, would add considerable fuel to the smouldering fire.

Perón may have yielded to pressure exerted on him by his former comrades-in-arms. Or, more likely, he realized he had nothing to gain politically from his wife's elevation to the vice presidency, since her usefulness to him did not depend on any official position she might have, but rather upon her status as his wife. The military's intransigence toward Evita furnished him with a convenient excuse to deny her the prize she desperately wanted.

The president did nothing to stop the "open meeting," which assembled a crowd estimated at two million in downtown Buenos Aires. Evita's arrival, fifteen minutes after the proceedings had begun, provoked a delirious response from the faithful.

The woman who mounted the platform was a far cry from the glamor queen of the "Rainbow Tour." The blonde curls and gaudy attire had long since given way to what one author has called "the streamlined, eternally classic style which was to be hers —and uniquely hers at that time—until her death." Her hair was drawn back severely, accentuating the growing gauntness of her features. Tears flooded her eyes, and a look of uncertainty clouded her expression.

A taped record of the proceeding has survived. It conveys a sense of drama far exceeding any staged or filmed version of her life. Her speech was brief and explosive, a classic in its rhythmic cadences, violent imagery, and naked passion. The ravages of illness hoarsened her voice to a lower, more theatrical pitch, and the fires within her invested that voice with a chilling power.

But her discourse was also totally inappropriate to the occasion. She said nothing about the vice presidency, but instead touched upon the usual themes—inordinate praise of her husband, revilement of the oligarchy, reference to herself as a "humble woman." Her hyperbole reached its zenith in the peroration, when she invoked her "spiritual authority" to proclaim Perón the victor in the coming elections.

The president then spoke briefly, again omitting mention of the Peronist ticket that would appear on the ballots. The crowd became restless and began to shout for Evita. Although organization and tight control had characterized every mass meeting staged in Argentina since Perón's inauguration, this one seemed on the verge of getting out of hand.

As the audience pressed Evita for an answer to their offer of the vice presidency, a sense of helplessness enveloped the First Lady. As she tried to respond, her voice broke and she seemed to be losing her composure. Perón snarled an order that the meeting be closed. Finally Evita announced that she would give an answer in a radio broadcast that night, and the multitude dispersed.

The answer did not come for nine days. Then, in a broadcast on the evening of August 31, Evita announced her "irrevocable and definite decision" to decline the nomination and remain at the side of Perón, to whom she would continue to convey "the hopes of the people." From that time on, August 31 became known, among the Peronist faithful, as the "Day of the Renunciation."

In the last week of September, two virtually simultaneous events shook Argentina. The military staged a coup designed to overthrow Perón, and Evita suffered a physical collapse. The armed uprising aborted shortly after it began, and at the same moment the government press office released the first bulletin informing the public that the First Lady was seriously ill.

Though confined to her bed, Evita summoned labor leaders and the minister of war and ordered the procurement of weapons that would be distributed to workers' militias to be formed for the defense of Perón. Money from the Eva Perón Foundation would be diverted to purchase automatic weapons from the Netherlands.

Evita's initiative sparked another of the myths, that of "Evita the Guerrilla." Her gesture was seen as proof of a class-conscious realization that the future of Peronism depended upon total identification with the needs and aspirations of workers, and that when push came to shove, they alone could be trusted to fight for Perón. But no workers' militias were ever organized. Perón was a military man at heart and could never do anything that might one day destroy the Army, an institution that had nurtured him during the formative stages of his life. The presence of armed workers, moreover, would upset the delicate balance of power that he alone was able to manipulate.

On November 3 Perón brought his wife to a hospital built by the Eva Perón Foundation, and three days later a cancer specialist from New York performed surgery on her. Although Juan Perón won reelection handily on November 11, the precarious state of the First Lady's health totally preoccupied loyal Peronists.

On the same day that Evita entered the hospital, a bomb shattered the showcase of an Argentine publishing house. The target of the attack was a display of a new book, *La razón de mi vida* (translated as *My Mission in Life* by a New York subsidy press that later put out an English-language edition). It purported to be the autobiography of Eva Perón.[13]

The inspiration for Evita's literary endeavor came from Manuel Penella de Silva, a Spanish journalist whose political views were somewhat unorthodox, especially in the context of the time. He blamed the excesses of Nazism on the absence of any female influence within Hitler's regime. He was also convinced that women could be humanity's salvation, not by competing with men for political power and adopting masculine traits, as he felt had occurred in the Anglo-Saxon world, but rather by bringing what he saw as feminine virtues to bear upon policy formulation. This could be accomplished by the creation of consultative, moderating legislative bodies composed entirely of women.

When he heard about Eva Perón, Penella de Silva made his way to Argentina and succeeded in gaining an introduction to her and winning her confidence. Concluding that she shared his views about women, he begged her to let him ghost-write her autobiography. The project appealed to her, and she obtained her husband's approval.

The diminutive, chain-smoking Spaniard shadowed Evita in her daily round of activities and drew from her the story of her life as she wished it to be told. His access to her provoked the enmity of some of her sycophantic followers, who ceaselessly conspired to oust him from their midst. Despite these obstacles, he managed to produce a draft. As one account puts it, "When he began...to read his manuscript to her, Evita cried as though it were a romance novel [and blurted] 'That's just the way it was.'"

Perón's reaction, however, was unequivocally negative. The Spaniard's vision of women in politics did not comport with the president's notions on the subject. He turned the text over to several of Evita's intimates, who proceeded to rewrite it. They not only purged it of the distinctive features Penella de Silva had added, but also incorporated extravagant references to Perón.

The style of *My Mission in Life* has nothing in common with that of the letter Evita wrote to Perón just before she left for Europe. The sentences are short and at times epigramatic, the paragraphs similarly succinct and the language less passionate. The impression is of Evita as she might want to be, rather than of Evita as she was.

The book blends a number of elements, such as:

AUTOBIOGRAPHICAL SNIPPETS, including Eva's attraction to public recitation even as a child, along with her feeling that, "I have a special inherent tendency to feel injustice with unusual and painful intensity..."

ADULATION OF PERÓN, that extended to comparing him with both Christ and Alexander the Great

SENTIMENT, that led to purple prose comparing the feelings that Argentines would have when Evita died with the sense of loss at the death of a mother

RESENTMENT, "Nothing belonging to the oligarchy can be good!"

SHEER NONSENSE, including her argument that a particular line of reasoning must be true, "first, because General Perón has said so, and secondly, because it is actually the truth."

The only trace of Penella de Silva's peculiar brand of feminism comes in select passages referring to the absence of women in the world's centers of power. Elsewhere, Evita is made to mouth antifeminist notions such as the old chestnut that a woman's place is in the home.

The book recognizes that some might argue feminism's incompatability with Peronism. After all, Evita had declared in a 1949 speech to women delegates at a national convention of Peronists: "For women to be a Peronist means above all total loyalty to Perón, subordination to Perón and blind faith in Perón." In *My Mission in Life* she admits that feminists might think it odd to organize a women's movement on the basis of the superiority of a particular man, but she argues that the case of Juan Perón falls in a different category.

In perhaps the most memorable lines of *My Mission in Life,* Evita characterizes herself as a sparrow, her husband as a condor who flies close to God: "All that I am, all that I have, all that I think and all that I feel, belongs to Perón." Although it is easy to dismiss this as the overheated rhetoric of a ghost-writer, the dedication Evita inscribed in her own hand in the copy of *La razón de mi vida* she gave to Perón conveys similar sentiments, creating the impression of a teenager's worship of a teacher with whom she had become infatuated.[14]

The Peronist propaganda machine immediately hailed the book as a masterpiece. Critics in the controlled press extolled its literary merits. A group of writers petitioned the Ministry of Education to award the author a "Grand Prize of Honor." Copies of the book—paperbacks for the masses, deluxe editions for the Peronist elite—poured from the nation's printing presses. It became a required text in Argentine schools.

Eva Perón did not recuperate well from her surgery. On March 6, 1952, Perón told the American ambassador that an anemia accompanied by a persistent low fever was complicating her recovery; her weight had fallen from 128 to 112 pounds; and she was also having kidney problems. Evita, he added, did not have the type of constitution that could easily fight off illness. In April a cabinet minister was reported as noting that "Evita is unable to sleep well at all, and arises at odd hours—from four o'clock on she is holding early morning audiences…The general described her as being bone-thin and 'as green as spinach.'"

On May Day, Evita gave what would be a farewell performance from the balcony of the Government House. Perón had to support her. Photos make him look as though he were holding a doll in his hands. She made a short speech laden with violent rhetoric aimed at her husband's enemies, whom she threatened with destruction at the hands of the "*descamisados* of the fatherland" if they ever dared to "lift a hand against Perón." In her peroration, she claimed that her role was to be a "rainbow arc of love between the people and Perón," a metaphor oddly incongruent amidst the dark threats she had just issued.

By May 7, her thirty-third birthday, her weight had dropped to 81 pounds. A steady stream of visitors passed through the residence to convey their best wishes. Everyone wanted to pose for pictures with her. The unspoken assumption was that this might be their last chance.

On inauguration day, June 4, despite the brisk, cold weather, Evita insisted on attending the ceremonies. She had to be injected with a painkilling drug. A brace was fashioned to fit under her long fur coat and enable her to stand next to her husband during an open-car ride. She endured the afternoon chill and saluted the crowds. It was to be her last public appearance. When the day was over, she retired to bed. She would not leave her sickroom alive.

Youth, glamor, adulation, agony, and premature death— Evita's tragic fate fed Argentina's lust for sentimentality like nothing else in the country's history. As the end approached a mass psychosis seemed to grip the country. There was an outpouring of gifts believed to have curative powers. Charms, holy water, sacred bones, and objects of every description arrived daily at the presidential residence. Hundreds of people gathered nearby in round-the-clock prayer vigils. Those who hated her also made their presence felt. On a wall in downtown Buenos Aires someone scribbled the inscription "Long live cancer!"

She finally died on July 26. The funeral ceremonies, described by one anti-Peronist writer as a "bachanal of necrophilia," took two weeks. The Spanish cultural attaché, who happened to be a physician specializing in the preservation of human bodies, then began the process of embalming Evita's remains.

The first mention of a "new book" by Evita appeared in a newspaper article three days after her death. At a mass meeting on October 17, 1952, Perón read aloud a document entitled "My Supreme Will," purportedly written by his late wife. In it, Eva specified that she wanted "all my rights, as the author of *La razón de mi vida* and *Mi mensaje*, when published, to be...considered the absolute property of Juan Perón and the Argentine people." Two weeks later a Peronist magazine reported that the "Will" was a chapter from *Mi mensaje*.

The existence of an unpublished Evita manuscript then seemed to fade from the Peronist consciousness. It was not until 1970 that another mention of it surfaced, this time in *La vida de Eva Perón: Tomo 1 — Testimonios para su historia (The Life of Eva Perón: Testimony for Her History)*, by Otelo Borroni and Robert Vacca. This was a serious effort to combine a biographical narrative with excerpts from interviews with people who knew or otherwise had contact with Evita, as well as from other sources. According to Borroni and Vacca, "Despite the condition of her health and when the doctors permitted it, Eva Perón wrote *Mi mensaje*, a book she did not succeed in completing."[15]

In 1979 a monograph about Evita (*Eva Perón: The Myths of a Woman*, by J. M. Taylor) made a brief, passing reference to it. A year later, the Fraser-Navarro biography also alluded to the book, and noted that "It was most probably, like her last speeches, a dissertation on the greatness of Perón and a ferocious attack on his enemies, particularly the Army, which had now taken the Oligarchy's place in Evita's mind as the most serious threat to Perón."

The document that eventually surfaced in 1987 and that was published under the title *Mi mensaje* came from the archives of Jorge Garrido, Argentina's chief notary during the Perón presidencies.

When the military ousted Perón in 1955, Garrido packed up a trove of documents, both official and unofficial, from the Government House and brought them to his home in a middle-class neighborhood near the Plaza Italia in downtown Buenos Aires, where he converted his garage into a storage area for them.[16] When he died, his family decided to try to sell the collection, which included the manuscript of *Mi mensaje*. An auction house consulted Fermín Chávez, a Peronist historian, about the document's authenticity, which he verified.

The manuscript was typed on stationery engraved with the name "Eva Perón" (although it does not bear the Peronist seal, which adorns the tops of the pages of her contemporaneous handwritten letters that have survived). Every page is initialed "E.P." in script that appears identical to the handwriting of Evita's letters (but would be easy to forge).

Any inquiry into the genuineness of the manuscript must begin with an appreciation of Evita's health when she was supposed to have written the book. Between March and June of 1952, the best guess for an appropriate time frame, she was in the throes of extreme physical agony, which required her to take strong analgesics. In addition, one of her physicians has stated that tranquilizers were given to her to permit her to rest, since she was also going through periods of overexcitement. Even though she had long periods of total lucidity, she was simply too weak, physically, to have expended the effort that would have been necessary to write a lengthy document in her own hand.

Yet given her extraordinary willpower, it is conceivable that over an extended period of time Evita may have dictated some farewell thoughts that could have been turned into a book. If so, how much of "My Message" reflects the actual words Evita said to the person or persons who were taking down the dictation?

The book could not possibly be a verbatim transcript, especially if she expressed her thoughts orally the way she conveyed them in handwritten letters. The holographic Evita epistles that have survived feature a stream-of-consciousness prose, completely unlike the style of "My Message." The letter she sent to Perón upon her departure to Europe is one example. A letter written to her husband apparently at the time of her operation (and thus not long before she may have dictated *Mi mensaje*) provides another. In it she declared: "Tonight I want to leave you this perfume above all else so that you will know I adore you and if it is possible today more than ever[,] because when I was suffering I felt your affection and goodness so much that until the last moment of my life, I will offer [mispelled] it to you body and soul, since you know I am hopelessly in love with my dear old man, well, since I knew [mispelled] you it was the Day of the Kings [January 6, the celebration of the visit of the Magi to Bethlehem, the holiday when children in the Spanish-speaking world receive presents] I am so happy with you that I'm afraid I don't deserve it, but I want you to know that in the world there can't be a woman who loves her husband as much as I love you." Two other handwritten letters Eva wrote during her final illness demonstrate the same meandering prose suffused with overripe phrases that seem to have come straight from the melodramas she used to broadcast.

There are other compelling reasons why the book cannot be entirely the work of Eva Perón. The sentence and paragraph structures of "My Message" and *My Mission in Life* are quite similar, and we know for a fact that others wrote the latter book, whose contents Eva merely ratified. Moreover, "My Message" contains literary allusions to Dante and the gospel, and a historical reference to the Middle Ages, which someone else must have supplied. Finally, Evita was surely incapable of organizing a manuscript in a coherent or even semi-coherent fashion, given the state of her health and her limited education.

Yet there are enough elements of pure Evita to suggest that, unlike *My Mission in Life*, "My Message" in part came directly from the First Lady. They include: the Manichaean division between good people (read Peronists) and bad (read anti-Peronists); the extolling of the virtues of fanaticism; the characterization of her enemies as cold and lacking in smell or taste; and the recognition of "two words as the favorite daughters of my heart: hate and love."

"My Message" could have originated in some of Evita's spoken words, as organized, amplified, and polished by one or more ghost-writers. But did she in fact dictate anything during her final months? There are two witnesses who have given testimony to support an answer in the affirmative.

Juan Jiménez Domínguez has claimed that he was the person to whom the First Lady dictated the bulk of the manuscript. In an undated interview published in a second edition of *Mi mensaje* he supplied very few details and no specific dates.[17] A totally devoted follower who first met Evita before her marriage to Perón, he numbered himself among those who believe that Eva was a "saint" and that Peronism was a "religion," a confession that may affect his credibility.

The most reliable testimony establishing that Evita did indeed dictate a manuscript during this period comes from Antonio Cafiero. Cafiero was a Catholic nationalist whose links to Peronism were first forged at the University of Buenos Aires, where he studied economics and was active in student politics. After graduation, he served several years in the Argentine embassy in Washington, and then he returned home to become Perón's Minister of Foreign Commerce at the tender age of twenty-nine.

Cafiero visited Evita several times during her final illness. One of these visits occurred on June 24. She expressed her concerns about members of the Catholic hierarchy, whom she suspected of plotting against Perón. The fact that Cafiero was a practicing Catholic who had been active in organizations with ties to the Church seems to have motivated the First Lady to express her hope that he would remain faithful to Perón. In an interview in Washington on June 10, 1996, he described the scene: "She was very weak and was sitting on the bed. Suddenly she got up, walked across the room, pulled a manuscript out from a drawer and began to read it to me." Cafiero remembers that it contained strong language condemning certain clerics and military officers. In his book *Desde que grité: ¡Viva Perón!* (*From the Time I Shouted Long Live Perón!*), published in 1983, he noted: "It seems to me that she poured all this into a book, or a book project that she was never able to complete." The passage of time made it impossible for him to be able to say with certainty whether what he heard the First Lady read was textually identical to *Mi mensaje*. Later that day she telephoned him at home to express her apology for doubting his loyalty.

Cafiero is an eminently credible witness. After Evita's death, Perón appointed him Minister of the Economy, and when the President quarreled bitterly with the Church in 1954, he resigned from the cabinet as a matter of conscience. Yet he remained a Peronist and in Perón's good graces. His political career has had remarkable longevity, and he most recently has been serving as president of the Argentine Senate.

Thus, the weight of the evidence strongly suggests that during the last months of her life Evita was giving dictation that could have become a manuscript. But to what extent does "My Message" convey the sense of what she said? An answer to this question requires a close look at the substance, as opposed to the style, of the document.

For example, Evita's denunciation of anti-Peronist elements within the military is certainly consistent with what she is known to have felt toward the Argentine Armed Forces. She was fully aware of how a number of officers felt toward her while she was living with Perón. Her paramour's arrest and the dangers he faced at the hands of his comrades-in-arms in October 1945 were not something she could readily forgive or forget. Their intransigent opposition to her vice-presidential ambitions and the coup attempt of September 1951 fed high-octane fuel to the antimilitary flames that burned within her.

But despite her rancor toward anti-Peronist elements within the officer corps, she had never before explicitly singled out the military for public condemnation, even in the speeches she delivered during the last months of her life. In those orations she had used violent, apocalyptical rhetoric against those who might harm her husband. She had referred to them as "vipers," and threatened to mobilize Argentine women, who would not "leave standing a single brick that was not Peronist," and "take justice into our own hands." Yet she refrained from saying that some of the "vipers" wore military uniforms.

"My Message" is significant because in it she openly attacked the military in unequivocally harsh language. This could not have pleased her husband, who had always felt a strong institutional loyalty toward the Army, despite the problems he had with members of its upper echelons. This fortifies the hypothesis that it was he who vetoed publication of the book. The fact that Garrido found the manuscript in the Government House would support the supposition that the president maintained control over it and kept it under wraps until his ouster in 1955.

A second distinctive feature of "My Message" is the denunciation of high clerics accused of plotting against Perón. In none of her public utterances had Evita ever pointed a finger of recrimination at the hierarchy. Under the Argentine Constitution, Roman Catholicism enjoyed the status of a state religion, and the president of the Republic had to be a Catholic. The Church exerted a strong influence over Argentine society. Any criticism of the upper echelons of the institution by a figure as powerful as Evita would have had significant repercussions. (Indeed, if Evita's sisters are devout Catholics, their desire to suppress her negative comments about the hierarchy might explain why they have disavowed the authenticity of "My Message.")

Perón had always stressed that papal encyclicals inspired and informed his social doctrine. Moreover, the Catholic bishops had indirectly supported him in the 1946 campaign by instructing the faithful that they could not in conscience vote for a candidate who advocated the banning of religious teaching in public schools. (Perón's opponent favored abolition, while Perón opposed it.)

But in late 1950, the president gave signs of being careless about his relations with the Church. He sent a message of greetings to a spiritist religious sect holding a Buenos Aires rally with the theme "Jesus Christ is not God." He also absented himself from the capital just as a papal legate was arriving on his way to a national eucharistic congress in the interior, and Evita had to make a face-saving appearance at its closing ceremony.

Evita had married Perón in the Church and professed a belief in Catholicism throughout her life. A Jesuit, Father Hernán Benítez, had known Evita since her actress days and served as the First Lady's confessor and confidant until the day of her death. Visiting the pope in Rome was one of the high points of the "Rainbow Tour." Every facility built by her Foundation had a Catholic chapel.

In *My Mission in Life* she called herself a Christian and a Catholic and strongly invoked her religious faith as justifying her concern for the poor, whom she identified with Christ. "I do not call on God very often," she noted, "but my love of Christ is much greater than you would think: I love him in the *descamisados*." These were words written by another, but they undoubtedly expressed her sentiments.

An undated, handwritten letter she penned not long before her death gives a more genuine indication of how she felt about religion. In it she commented that "I never kept benches in Churches warm,"[18] and went on to say that she felt closer to the Lord by aiding the poor and the sick, and by struggling on behalf of workers.

"My Message" carries these sentiments further by faulting the hierarchy "for having betrayed Christ, who was compassionate with the masses…" Asserting that she was not against the clergy or against the Catholic religion, Evita praised the humble priests who worked with the poor, and stressed the compatibility of Catholic doctrine with service to the common people. Indeed, by emphasizing the need for the Church to exercise an option for the poor, the text emits strong echoes of liberation theology.

However difficult it may be to believe that Evita could have anticipated a Catholic movement that did not emerge until the 1960s, her sympathies certainly tended in its direction. It is well within the range of possibility that her calls for Catholicism to commit itself wholeheartedly to the underprivileged classes amounted to orthodox Peronism pushed beyond its bounds by Evita's passionate identification with her *descamisados*.

A clue to how references to Catholicism may have entered the text may be found in the peculiar, and somewhat misleading, mention of León Bloy in the chapter entitled "My Supreme Will."

There Evita proclaimed: "God will not let me lie if I repeat at that moment one more time, like León Bloy, that I cannot imagine heaven without Perón." This was in fact an allusion to a passage from *My Mission in Life* in which Evita claimed to have read León Bloy's book on Napoleon, in which Bloy wrote that he could not conceive of heaven without his Emperor. "I liked this, and in a speech said that neither could I imagine Heaven without Perón."

León Bloy, a Roman Catholic convert whose life spanned from 1846 to 1917, was a French novelist, polemicist, and critic who preached spiritual revival through suffering and destitution. He believed that the Holy Spirit could bring redemption and open mankind to the hidden language of the universe. He was the mentor of Jacques Maritain, an influential Catholic philosopher who was much in vogue in certain Argentine intellectual circles at that time.

The notion of Evita reading a book by León Bloy is far-fetched, to say the least. One of the persons suspected of writing the final version of *My Mission in Life* was Raul Mendé, an ex-seminarian who might have been familiar with Bloy. It would be a safe guess that he might have had something to do with the reappearance of Bloy's name in the text of "My Message". He would then have probably been the author of Evita's exigesis on Catholic doctrine.

The idea of chastising the hierarchy may have been Evita's idea (or Perón himself may have inspired it as a way to nip in the bud any ecclesiastical involvement in conspiracies against him). Some of the fervor that went into these criticisms may have carried over to Evita's comments about Catholicism and the poor.

A third distinctive feature of "My Message" is that some of the words and phrases in the document have what might seem to be a leftist ring. There are denunciations of "imperialisms" and more specifically "capitalist imperialism" ("I have seen its miseries and its crimes up close"). There are constant references to the "people" (by which she meant the "common people"), the "enemies of the people," the "hour of the people," "serving the people," *et cetera*, all phrases that appear prominently in the Marxist lexicon. Even though the text disavows class struggle as such, it calls for the building of a society based upon a single class (or a classless society, which presumably could not be achieved without some sort of struggle).

This language, however, also reflects orthodox Peronism, which consistently maintained that it served the interests of the common people. The essence of the doctrine preached by Perón was that it offered a middle way between the extremes of capitalism and communism, and that it sought to achieve in Argentina a society that was "socially just, economically free and politically independent."

Moreover, Perón's criticisms of capitalist imperialism did not mean he was any less averse to communist imperialism (which explains why the word, when used in a derogatory sense, often appeared in the plural), but instead reflected his concern with the immediate impacts of American foreign policy upon Argentina.

The views of the class struggle, as expressed in the final section of "My Message," are actually quite similar to words put in Evita's mouth by the authors of *My Mission in Life*. There, Evita was made to call for an end to class struggle, and a spirit of cooperation between employers and laborers. She went on to postulate that "Our aim is that workers earn enough to live honestly, like human beings, and that the masters also be content to gain enough to maintain industry and progress and live worthily." Thus, the Peronist ideal was for employers and employees to work in harmony toward a common goal (in what Perón liked to call the "organized community"). But Evita confessed that she did not always agree with the notion of an "exact balance of justice," because she felt the scales should be tipped in favor of the workers.

"My Message" seems to go a bit beyond this by suggesting that the oligarchy should become "of our class and of our race. How? By making them work…[since] when everyone lives off their own work, and not off someone else's, we will all be better…" But under a less radical interpretation of this language, it could amount to a denunciation of the idle rich, not private employers who owned their own businesses and paid their workers decent wages.

"My Message" contains not only leftist-sounding words and phrases, but also violent rhetoric that vaguely suggests social revolution, in Argentina as well as elsewhere. Thus, if "the armed forces of the world" do not put the happiness of the people first, "the people themselves, with their own hands, in full consciousness of our invincible power, will erase them from the history of humankind." Even more ominous is the following declaration: "[The military] could defeat us in one day...at night or by surprise...but if the next day we take to the street, or refuse to work, or sabotage everything they want to order, they will have to resign themselves to giving freedom and justice back to us."

Adding the incendiary language in Evita's last speeches to selected passages from "My Message" provides grist for those who believe that Eva Perón was a crypto-revolutionary. The myth of "Evita the Guerrilla" has a long and interesting history.

During the years of Juan Perón's exile in Spain (1960–1973), the Cuban revolution attracted young people all over Latin America to left-wing ideologies that saw socialism as the only solution to the political, economic, and social underdevelopment that afflicted the continent. Argentina was no exception. However, the Argentine working class, in whose name the youthful rebels would have liked to have been able to speak, was still firmly committed to the Peronist cause. This convinced many of the new radicals to identify themselves with what they claimed was the revolutionary essence of Peronism.

Perón encouraged this by making occasional incendiary utterances. However, his actual motivation was to utilize what came to be known as the Peronist Youth to help create instability in Argentina, and force the military to permit his return as a way to preserve social peace. In the end, this turned out to be a brilliant tactic, demonstrating the triumph of Perón's cynicism over the naiveté of the young people who were trying to co-opt him.

As part of their effort to revolutionize Peronism, youthful Argentines constructed the myth of a revolutionary Eva Perón. If she had not died, they repeated over and over again, she would be with them in the trenches, even to the point of supporting them in the perpetration of revolutionary violence against capitalist oppression. They often cited her call for the organization of armed workers' militias to defend Perón against his enemies in the Armed Forces. "Evita the Guerrilla" became one of their emblems, as they chanted her name and plastered her likeness on their posters. After her death, they even kidnapped and murdered the ex-president responsible for shipping Evita's corpse out of Argentina, and four years later stole *his* body from its grave and held it hostage until the government brought *her* body back to Argentina.

This effort to appropriate Evita became part of what eventually became a bloody struggle between the left and right wings of the Peronist movement over the symbols of Peronism. Since the common people of Argentina still venerated Eva Perón, the faction establishing her as one of their own could exert a powerful hold over the Peronist masses.

Although the right prevailed over the left when Perón returned to Argentina and abandoned the young militants who had helped pave the way for his amazing political comeback, the battle to claim Evita continues. In one of the essays accompanying the 1994 edition of *Mi mensaje*, the author avers that the text is consistent with revolutionary Peronism, and makes the claim that "Eva intuitively agreed with Karl Marx."

Evita always followed the ideological line laid down by her husband. Most of the revolutionary language of "My Message" may be interpreted as being consistent with Perón's own views, which if nothing else were highly flexible and adaptable to any circumstance or necessity. To the extent that "My Message" may depart somewhat from what Perón said or wrote, two hypotheses may be offered: Evita may indeed have expressed these thoughts, or someone else doctored the text to make it lean to the left.

It is, of course, conceivable that Evita may have dictated some or all of the words that make her sound like a revolutionary. Passion governed everything she did. The first armed military uprising against her husband might have swept her to an emotional extreme that made her say what she said. An alternative (and to some extent contradictory) explanation is that for the first time in her life she was placed under confinement and could not live her customary hyperactive life. With time to reflect, and with the specter of death hanging over her, she may well have entertained thoughts that went beyond the orthodox Peronism she had always mouthed. Moreover, it is possible to read most of what she may have said as within the parameters of her husband's malleable doctrine.

It is, of course, conceivable that the revolutionary rhetoric, in whole or in part, may have entered the text at a later point. However, the arguments against the doctoring of the text to give it a leftist spin seem persuasive. If someone wanted to do this, he or she would have made the language more explicitly radical, so that there would be little doubt where Evita stood on the ideological spectrum. If the doctoring had occurred during the 1960s or 1970s, those responsible would surely have found some way to make the document public, since it was in their vital interest to establish that Evita was one of them. From 1955 on, the manuscript seems to have been in the exclusive possession of Jorge Garrido, who did not have ties to the left. Finally, it is difficult to believe that an Argentine leftist embarked on this endeavor would have made the mistake of attributing to Lenin, rather than Marx, the aphorism that "religion is the opiate of the people," as was done in the published text of *Mi mensaje*.

Another peculiar feature of "My Message" is the penultimate section entitled "My Supreme Will," which Perón read aloud on October 17, 1952. Evita left behind two letters she wrote by hand just before her death. One of them, dated June 29, 1952, contains a single page and is incomplete. This document comprises the first couple of paragraphs of "My Supreme Will," and is a fraction of the text made public by her husband. The other, undated and self-characterized as "my last will," is a rambling text in Evita's style of writing. As the Fraser-Navarro biography points out, the sentiments of the second letter "are quite different [from those expressed in "My Supreme Will"] and could be those of another person."

In her "last will" letter, Evita expressed her undying love for Perón and the common people of Argentina, denounced unnamed traitors and military officers, and asked God to protect workers, old people, women, and children from exploitation at the hands of "scoundrels."

The letter concluded with her wishes about the disposition of her earthly goods, in prose so opaque as to be nearly incomprehensible: "I want everything I have there is no other heir than Perón [sic]…and that the General keep the jewels that the General gave me and the workers [gave me and that] each of my sisters and my mother be given one of them as a souvenir and the rest they give to the Foundation so that [the wealth that] was given to me with love with that same love may serve to alleviate grief and stop the bleeding of wounds[;] I ask the general to give Mama 3,000 pesos a month while she lives[, and] let him not forget *Doña Juana* [Evita's mother] whom I can't forget."

The "Supreme Will" read by Perón and included as a section in "My Message" makes no mention of Evita's family. This is a significant omission that casts considerable doubt upon its authenticity, and marks it as a public rather than a personal document.

In addition, the "Supreme Will" does not contain the sort of prose Evita wrote, or the type of language she generally used. Even the few paragraphs in her own hand are stylistically different from what appears in her genuine letters, and might have been dictated to her. If so, the person who most logically would have told her what to write was her husband. Moreover, the flowery phrases and extravagant praise heaped upon Perón in "My Supreme Will" had to have come from someone other than Evita, perhaps the same person or persons who put together the final version of "My Message."

The "Supreme Will" left all Eva's property, including the royalties from *My Mission in Life* and "My Message," to Perón, to do with as he pleased, even to the extreme of destroying everything. "But after Perón, the only heir to my belongings must be the people…" The testament then asked that the estate be used for the creation of a new foundation that would provide a number of enumerated social benefits for the *descamisados* and their children. If there was an apparent contradiction between specifying that the entire estate pass to Perón and at the same time that a foundation be set up from its proceeds, the best explanation for the incongruity is that it permitted Perón to take at least partial credit for the creation of the new entity. The fact that the intended beneficiaries never received more than a fraction of what Eva had supposedly bequeathed them has never detracted from the myth of "Evita the Good."

Presenting this as Evita's "Supreme Will" at a mass rally on October 17, 1952, was sheer theater. The document did not comply with formalities required by Argentine law—for instance, there were no witnesses to it—and hence it was not legally valid. Under the law, Evita's estate should have passed in equal shares to her husband and her mother.

These technicalities did not go unnoticed. Two days before Perón presented Evita's "Supreme Will" to the public, her mother put her signature to a document legally ceding to her son-in-law all her legal rights to Eva's estate. She received nothing in return. According to allegations made in a lawsuit brought by Juana Ibarguren in 1960 against Perón and claiming that she had signed against her will, the president sent emissaries to try to convince her to sign over her rights, but she refused; finally, Perón had Eva's brother Juan, who served as his private secretary, go to his mother and beg her to sign; he told her that if she didn't, his life would be at risk and he would have to flee the country.[19] The lawsuit finally came to an end in 1972, after the death of Eva's mother, when a court awarded Eva's two surviving sisters a judgment against Perón.[20]

The inescapable conclusion to be drawn from the text of "My Supreme Will," as illuminated by the handwritten "last will" letter and the subsequent struggle over the estate, is that this chapter does not really represent Evita's wishes for the disposition of her property. Since it was dated June 29, at that time she may have been too weak to resist its composition, as the Fraser-Navarro biography suggests.

One final unique aspect of "My Message" merits mention. At certain points Evita no longer seems the humble, self-effacing woman she comes across as in *My Mission in Life*. In the latter, Perón is a condor and she is a "sparrow in an immense flock of sparrows." "My Message" has Evita accompanying her husband in flight. In *My Mission in Life* Perón is the "figure" and Evita the "shadow." In "My Message" Evita admits that she once resigned herself to being "[n]estled in a corner of my Colonel's life…like a bouquet of flowers in his house," but describes how she shielded her husband and ejected enemies from his inner circle. It also contains bits of self-promotional exaggeration, such as the statements that "Every country in the world paid homage to me, in some respect," and "I now know all the truths and all the lies of the world."

Moreover, at the very outset of the text she pointed out that "*My Mission in Life* didn't manage to say all that I feel and think," and was a "disorganized mix of feelings and thoughts." This is a remarkable admission, in light of the reverence with which Peronists received the book.

These elements of "My Message" bear the unmistakable ring of the real Evita. Although she truly felt adulation for Perón, she must have realized in her heart that she had made a vastly significant contribution to his success. On her deathbed she had time to think, and it is not surprising that she might have wanted to express for posterity her personal views about her career at Perón's side.

But the president had his own political reasons for not wanting the full text of "My Message" to be published. He preferred to deal with the military in his own way, which did not include heaping invective upon the upper level of the officer corps. He also saw no reason to instigate an open quarrel with the Roman Catholic hierarchy.[21] The only portion of the text advancing his interests was the "Supreme Will," which he did make public. Because it is written in the style of a letter, there is reason to doubt that it was truly meant to be a book chapter.

For anyone fascinated by the real Eva Perón, "My Message" is a vital document containing enough of Evita to suggest that it conveys a number of her thoughts as she lay dying. It would have been perfectly natural for her, at that point in time, to want to sound a clarion call against what she perceived as serious threats to Perón from military and ecclesiastical sources. She might well have wanted to clarify her place in history, so that the world would know what she considered the truth about the "someone" she had become.

Moreover, passages from "My Message" allow believers in the legendary Evita to fortify their preconceptions. With its expressions of concern for the fate of the downtrodden, the book has elements that enhance the myth of "Evita the Good," even though the raw emotion and violent language it conveys seem far from saintly. Similarly, the incendiary rhetoric flashing from it feeds into the myth of "Evita the Guerrilla," despite the difficulty of reconciling her total allegiance to Perón and his peculiar brand of populism with the proto-socialist ideas later attributed to her by the young revolutionaries of the 1960s and 1970s.

The book may even lend support to those of us who take the romantic view of Evita, which holds that she was a poor, uneducated, instinctive, emotionally volatile woman who put up a valiant struggle against class and gender bias; was artfully manipulated by her husband; yet grew into a political role she performed memorably within the limits of her capabilities and the space allotted to her.

1 In her book *My Mission in Life*, she explained that she considered herself "Eva Perón" only in her formal role as wife of the President, and preferred "Evita," which for her meant "a link stretched between the hopes of the people and the fulfilling hands of Perón." This Introduction will use the appellations "Evita," "Eva," "Eva Perón" and "First Lady" interchangeably, without intent to ascribe any special meaning to each.

2 Indeed, when President Perón more than twenty-five years later proposed legislation that would have given illegitimate children the same legal rights as offspring from legitimate marriages, the Roman Catholic hierarchy denounced it as an assault on the sanctity of the family and forced the withdrawal of the bill.

3 The epithet, as expressed in another nasty joke, found its way into the rock opera. When Eva complains, during her 1947 European tour, that hostile crowds in Rome were calling her a whore, one of her Italian escorts tells her not to feel bad, because "I'm still called an admiral/ Yet I gave up the sea long ago."

4 The source for this anecdote is *De Banda Pra Lua*, a memoir written by Aloysio de Oliveira, Carmen's bandleader. Later, when Carmen was a star in Hollywood and Eva the First Lady of Argentina, Carmen took a more benign view of her. She told her mother: "Mama, Evita came

to see *me!* Evita and I, we are alike: we both care for the poor." This anecdote appears in *Brazilian Bombshell: The Biography of Carmen Miranda*, by Martha Gil-Montero.

5   Perhaps the most fanciful and laughably apocryphal anecdote dating from this period appears in *The Aspirin Wars*, by Charles C. Mann and Mark Plummer. According to the authors, the export division of Sterling Drug Company "gave an unknown chanteuse named Maria Eva Duarte her first professional singing job. Duarte was fired when she got sick and didn't show up at the station." The government shut down the radio station and threatened to do the same to Sterling's subsidiary, until the latter's representatives realized "who she was" and implored Evita's forgiveness. She finally relented. "With Evita singing the jingles...Argentina became the biggest per capita consumer of aspirin in the world."

6   This was the title of an article that appeared in *Look* magazine on September 30, 1947.

7   Set in nineteenth-century Spain, the story line puts Eva in the role of a solitude-craving woman living with her servants in a mansion. A young engineer visits her and learns of her shady past. Born into a wealthy family, she married a French officer, who then killed himself for no apparent reason. Her fortune was running low, so she replenished it at the roulette table one night in Montecarlo. While traveling in Europe she posed (nude or nearly nude, it is suggested) for painters. She returned to Spain to live by herself and lavish presents and attention upon the peasants who work for her.

The engineer falls madly in love with her. But the people of the community become scandalized when he moves into her home. She attends church for the first time in four months, and the priest sermonizes against violations of God's law. Everyone knows to what he is referring. The bride of one of her peasants refuses to set foot in the mansion on her wedding day. Then the title character discovers that the money she has been living on and distributing generously was not hers but actually came from the pockets of her household servants, who were somehow giving it to her without her knowledge and now have nothing left, so she is totally impoverished. Distraught, she commits suicide.

A charitable assessment is that Eva Duarte was not a good movie actress. Miscast as an older woman, she moves stiffly and uncomfortably across the screen, and speaks in a high-pitched monotone.

The final print was not completed until Evita had become First Lady. The director presented it to Perón and his wife, and they decided against exhibiting it in public. The accepted version of events was that the print was eventually destroyed. However, in the mid-1980s, a print turned up in a safe in Montevideo, Uruguay.

8   In an interview with Tomás Eloy Martínez, Lilian Lagomarsino de Guardo, the First Lady's companion on the trip, described how difficult it was for Evita to write. "The poor thing would chew the wood of the pencil, entwine her legs against the seat, and not one word would come out."

9   The Spanish people were expressing gratitude for shipments of food Perón had sent to the country in the difficult postwar period when the international community was treating Spain as a pariah because of its ties to the Axis.

10 In *La pródiga*, the character Evita plays asks her lover whether he likes children. When he answers in the affirmative, she tells him, "I'll never have one."

11 This version appears in *The Perón Novel*, a fictional construct of Perón's life. Tomás Eloy Martínez, the author, later insisted in a February 1993 interview in the Argentine magazine *Somos* that it was based upon documentary evidence, in the form of a letter written by Aurelia to a cousin.

12 She is supposed to have been pregnant during the filming of *La pródiga*. Unnamed workers on the set have been quoted as saying that she would pat her stomach and say, "I have a little Perón here." The costumes she wore during the film would have covered up any pregnancy. The fact that her participation in the film ended abruptly in September (*La pródiga*'s ending does seem incomplete), when she supposedly was hospitalized and miscarried, would support the hypothesis of her pregnancy, but much more verification would be needed to establish it as a fact.

13 This would be the second book published in Evita's name. In 1951 she delivered a series of lectures at the Advanced School of Peronism. (According to one account, she never even looked at them beforehand and sight-read the text.) They later appeared in print under the title *Historia del Peronismo* (*The History of Peronism*).

14 A military officer who had somehow come into possession of this white-leather-bound copy of *La razón de mi vida* permitted me to look at it in 1984. The title page bore the stamped designation "001."

15 A book published one year later, *Eva Perón: ¿Aventurera o militante?* (*Eva Perón: Adventuress or Militant?*) by Juan José Sebreli mentioned in a chronology of Evita's life a "supposedly unpublished book, *Mi mensaje.*"

16 The retention of documents by government officials leaving office is quite common in Argentina and enormously complicates the work of researchers. In 1978 Garrido graciously let me visit his garage and peruse some of the material there, but I did not stumble across *Mi mensaje.*

17 A translation of a portion of the interview is included in this volume.

18 The phrase *calentar bancos* or *calentar sillas* (literally, to warm benches or seats) conveys the sense of boring a host with long visits. The family of a woman whose fiancé spends a good deal of time visiting her at home but never goes ahead with the marriage would use the expression to complain about him.

19 Juan was suspected of having used his office for personal gain. In 1953 he was found with a bullet in his head. An official investigation concluded that he had killed himself, but many suspected that he had been murdered.

20 Neither of Evita's "wills" mentioned the valuable real property she owned or the net worth of her entire estate, which turned out to be considerable. After a series of legal proceedings stretching over several decades, what she left behind was divided equally between her sisters and Isabel Perón, the third wife and widow of Juan Perón. Although there were many rumors about the existence of Swiss bank accounts in Evita's name, no such funds have ever surfaced.

21 Two year later, however, he would provoke the Church into a fight that weakened him and paved the way for his downfall, and Evita's words would become prophetic.

My Message

My Message

Recently, in the hours of my illness, I have thought often of this message from my heart.

Perhaps because I didn't manage to say all that I feel and think in *My Mission in Life*, I have to write again....

I left too many gaps that I should fill; and this time it isn't because I need to.

No. It might be better for me if I kept quiet, didn't say any of the things I am going to say and let everything I said in my first book stand as the definitive word.

But my love and my pain cannot settle for that disorganized mix of feelings and thoughts that I left in the pages of *My Mission in Life*.

I love the *descamisados*, the women, the workers of my people too much, and, by extension, I love all the world's exploited people, condemned to death by imperialisms and the privileges of land ownership, too much...

The suffering of the poor, the humble, the great pain of so much of humanity without sun and without sky hurts me too much to keep quiet.

If there are still shadows and clouds trying to cover the sky and the sun of our land—and there is still much pain to mitigate and so many wounds to stanch!— how will it be where no one has seen the light or held in his hands the flag of the people who march in silence, without tears or sighs, bleeding under the night of slavery..., and how will it be where the light can be seen, but too far away, and hope is an immense pain that rebels and burns in the flesh and soul of the people parched for liberty and justice...!

*

My Message is for them: for my people and for all of humanity's people.

I no longer want to explain my life or my work.

I no longer seek praise. I couldn't care less about the hatred or the praise of men who belong to the race of exploiters.

I want to incite the people. I want to ignite them with the fire of my heart. I want to tell them the truth that a humble woman from the country—the first woman of the people who would not let herself be dazzled by power or glory—learned in the world of those who rule and govern humanity's people.

I want to tell them the truth that no one has ever spoken, because no one was able to follow the farce the way I did, to learn the whole truth.

Because no one who left the people to take my path ever went back. They were dazzled by the marvelous fantasy of power, and they remained there to enjoy the lie.

I, too, wore all the honors of glory, of vanity, and of power. I let myself be adorned by the finest jewels on earth. Every country of the world paid homage to me, in some respect. Everything that the clique of men with whom I happened to live—as the wife of an extraordinary president—wanted to offer me, I accepted, with a smile, "using my face" to guard my heart. But smiling, in the middle of the farce, I learned the truth of all their lies.

I can now say how much they lie, all that they deceive, everything they pretend, because I know men in their greatness and in their misery.

*

Often, I have had before my eyes, at the same time, as if to compare them face to face, the misery of greatness and the greatness of misery.

I would not let the soul I brought from the street be yanked away....That is why I was never seduced by the grandeur of power, and I could see their misery; and that is why I never forgot my people's misery and why I could see their greatness.

I now know all the truths and all the lies of the world.

I have to tell them to the people from where I came. And I have to tell them to all the deceived people of humankind: to the workers, the women, the humble *descamisados* of my Nation, and to all the *descamisados* on earth—to the infinite race of the people!—as a message from my heart.

I Had to Fly with Him

In *My Mission in Life*, with my paltry words, I talked about the wonderful day of my existence when I met Perón.

He was already at battle.

I remember it as if I could see him now, with his sparkling eyes, his head held high, his clean smile, his words lit from the fire in his heart.

From the first moment, I saw the shadow of his enemies, stalking him like vultures from above or like vicious snakes from the beaten earth.

I thought Perón was too much alone, overly confident in the winning power of his ideals, believing the first thing anyone said as if it were his own generous and clean, sincere, and honorable words.

∗

I was not drawn by his stature or the honors of his
position—even less by his military stripes.

From the first moment, I saw his heart...and on top
of the pedestal of his heart, the mast of his ideals holding
the flag of his Nation and his People close to the sky.

I saw his immense solitude, like the solitude of the
condor, like that of the highest peaks, like the solitude
of stars in the immenseness of infinity.

And in spite of my smallness, I decided to
accompany him.

To follow him, to be with him, I would have been,
would have done anything—anything but change the
course of his destiny!

That was when I told him one day, "I am prepared
to follow you, wherever you go."

Little by little, I took on his battles, too.

Sometimes because his enemies provoked me.
Other times because I was outraged by their treachery
and their lies.

I had decided to follow Perón, but I was not
resigned to follow him from a distance, knowing that he
was surrounded by enemies and ambitious men, who
disguised themselves with friendly words—and by
friends who didn't feel even the heat of the shadow of
his ideals.

I wanted to spend the days and the nights of his
life with him, in the peace of his rests, and in the battles
of his fight.

I already knew that, like a condor, he was flying
high and alone...and yet I had to fly with him!

I admit that in the beginning I did not realize the magnitude of my decision…. I thought I could help Perón with my affection as a woman, with the company of my heart smitten by his person and his cause…but nothing more! I thought my task was to fill his loneliness with the joy and enthusiasm of my youth.

My Colonel

And so we embarked upon our journey, happy and joyful in the midst of the battle.

One day he confessed that I, his little *"giovinota,"* as he often called me, was the only loyal and sincere companion of his life.

Never had my smallness pained me as it did that day! And I decided I would do the impossible to be a better companion to him.

I remember asking him to be my teacher. In the respites of his fight, he would teach me a little of as much as I could learn.

I liked to read by his side. We started with Plutarch's *The Parallel Lives* and then moved on to *The Complete Letters of Lord Chesterfield to his son Stanhope.* In a short time, he taught me a little of the languages he knew: English, Italian, French.

Without realizing it, I was also learning, from his conversations, the history of Napoleon, of Alexander, and of all of history's great men.

And that is how he taught me to view our own history differently.

With him, I learned to read the panorama of domestic and international political questions.

He often spoke to me of his dreams and his hopes, his grand ideals.

Nestled in a corner of my Colonel's life, it strikes me that I was like a bouquet of flowers in his house. I never attempted to be more than that.

However…, the battle that broke out around Perón was too harsh, his enemies very strong, his loneliness almost infinite, and my love too great for me to resign myself to being nothing more than a touch of joy on "my Colonel's" path.

The First Shadows

Most of the men around Perón at that time considered me nothing but a simple opportunist.

They were mediocre, in the end…unlike me with my soul burning, they had not been able to feel the fire of Perón, of his greatness and of his goodness, of his dreams and of his ideals.

They thought I was "calculating" with Perón, because they were measuring with the paltry yardstick of their souls.

I got to know them close up, one by one. Later, almost every one of them betrayed Perón. Some in October of 1945; others later…, and I had the pleasure of insulting them to their faces, denouncing out loud the disloyalty and dishonor with which they proceeded, or fighting them until proving the hypocrisy of their actions and intentions.

I remained alone next to "my Colonel" until they took him prisoner.

From those days on, I distrusted upper-class friends and men of honor. And I clung blindly to the humble men and women of my people who, without so much "honor" and without so many "titles" or "privileges," know how to risk their lives for a man, for a cause, for an ideal...or for a simple feeling from the heart!

Those first great disappointments made me see my path clearly.

But I could not believe in anything or anyone who wasn't of his people.

Since then I have told him countless times in every tone of voice so that he'll never forget it, how, with so many words, the men who generally surround a president feign their honor and loyalty.

The peoples of the earth should not just elect the man who will lead them. They should know how to protect him from their enemies, who lurk in the antechambers of every government.

On behalf of my people, I protected Perón, and I ejected their enemies from the antechambers— sometimes with a smile and other times with the harsh words of the truth I spoke in their faces with all the indignation of my rebelliousness.

The People's Enemies

The people's enemies were and remain Perón's enemies.

I have seen them approach him with every kind of malice and lie.

I want to denounce them definitively.

Because they will be the eternal enemies of Perón and of the people, here and every place in the world where the flag of justice and liberty is raised.

We have defeated them, but they belong to a race that will never die definitively.

In our blood, we all have the seeds of selfishness that could turn us into enemies of the people and its cause.

We must squash it wherever it springs up...if we want the world one day to reach the bright noonday of the people. And if we do not want the night to fall again over their victory.

Perón's enemies...I have seen them up close and personal.

I never remained in the rearguard of his battles.

I was in the front line of combat, fighting the short days and the long nights of my zeal, infinite like the thirst of my heart. And I carried out two tasks— I don't know which was more worthy of a small life like mine, but my life in the end—one, to fight for the rights of my people, and the other, to watch Perón's back.

In this double duty, immense for me, armed with nothing but my ardent heart, I met the enemies of Perón and my people.

They are the same!

Yes! I never saw anyone from our race—the race of the people—fighting against Perón.

But I did see the others.

Sometimes I've seen them cold and insensitive. I swear with all the force of my fanaticism that they always revolted me. I have felt them cold like toads or snakes. The only thing that moves them is envy. There is no need to fear them. The envy of toads could never conceal the song of nightingales!

But we must move them off the road.

*

They cannot be near the people or the men whom the people elect to lead them.

And they definitely cannot be the leaders of the people.

The leaders of the people must be fanatics for the people.

If not, they grow dizzy at the top—and they do not return!

And I've seen them, too, with the dizziness of the heights of power.

Fanatics

Only fanatics—who are idealists and partisan—do not give up. The cold and indifferent should not serve the people, because they cannot even if they want to.

To serve the people, one has to be prepared for anything—including death.

The cold do not die for a cause, but only by accident. Fanatics do.

I like fanatics and all of history's fanaticisms. I like the heroes, the saints, the martyrs, whatever the cause and reason behind the fanaticism.

Fanaticism turns life into a permanent and heroic process of dying; but it is the only way that life can defeat death.

That is why I am fanatic. I would give my life for Perón and for the people…because I am sure that only by giving it will I win the right to live in them for all of eternity.

And fanatical is how I want the women of my people, the workers and the *descamisados* to be.

Fanaticism is the only force that God gave the heart to win its battles.

It is the great strength of the people: the only one that its enemies do not have, because they have abolished from the world everything that smacks of the heart.

That is why we will defeat them. They have money, privilege, hierarchy, power, and wealth…, but they can never be fanatics…because they have no heart. We do.

They cannot be idealists because ideas have their roots in intelligence, but ideals have their foundation in the heart.

They cannot be fanatics because shadows cannot see themselves in the mirror of the sun.

Face to face, they, with all the strength in the world, and we, with our fanaticism, we will always prevail.

We must convince ourselves once and for all. The world will belong to the people if the people decide to ignite in the sacred fire of our fanaticism, but igniting ourselves means burning, ignoring the siren of the mediocre, ignoring the imbeciles who speak to us of prudence.

Those who speak of sweetness and of love forget that Christ said, "I have come to bring fire over the earth and what I most want is that it burn!"

He gave us a divine example of fanaticism.

Next to him, what are the eternal preachers of mediocrity?

*

Neither Faithful nor Rebellious

I have measured the coldness and the fanaticism of men with the yardstick of my heart.

The two extremes have constantly marched past me. The landscape of these years of my life has been an intense contrast of lightness and darkness.

Every minute of my life I have thought about and suffered through that tremendous encounter between fanaticism and indifference.

I admit that the hatred of his enemies does not hurt me as much as the coldness and indifference of those who should be friends to Perón's wonderful cause.

I understand better, and I would almost be more forgiving of the oligarchy's hatred than the coldness of some bastard son of the people who neither feels nor understands Perón.

If there is one thing for which I reproach the high military and clerical hierarchies, it is precisely their coldness and indifference before the drama of my people. Yes. I am not exaggerating. What is happening to our people is a drama, an authentic and extra-ordinary drama for the ownership of life...of happiness...of the pure and simple well-being that my people have been dreaming about since the beginning of history.

The meeting of Perón and the People took place on October 17.

On that unforgettable night, the destiny of both was sealed, and the immense drama thus began...

Before a world of oppressed peoples, Perón raised the flag of our liberation.

Before a world of exploited peoples, Perón raised the flag of justice.

I added my heart and I intertwined the two flags of justice and liberty with a little love. But all this— liberty, justice, and love, Perón and his people—all this is too much to be treated with indifference or coldness.

All this deserves either love or hate.

The tepid, the indifferent, the mentally reserved, the quasi-Peronists make me sick.

They are repugnant because they lack smell or taste.

Before the constant and inexorable advance of the wonderful day of the people, men divide themselves into the three eternal camps of hatred, indifference, and love.

There are fanatics of the people.

There are enemies of the people.

And there are...the indifferent.

The latter belong to the class of men that Dante portrayed in the Gates of Hell.

They never risk anything.

They are like "the angels who were neither faithful nor rebellious."

Whoever May Fall

I have seen Perón fight tirelessly for his people against the dominating forces of humanity.

This chapter is dedicated to his people.

I cannot stifle it because that would be lying to my people and to all the peoples on earth who have suffered and who suffer under the merciless domination of imperialisms.

It is time to tell the truth, whatever the cost and whoever may fall.

In the world there are nations that exploit and there are nations that are exploited.

I wouldn't say anything if it were just about nations...but the thing is that behind every nation that imperialism oppresses, there is a people of slaves and exploited men and women.

And still the same imperialist nations always hide behind their grandeur and their tinsel [the bitter and harsh reality of an oppressed people].

Imperialisms have been and are the cause of the greatest misfortunes of humankind—of the humankind incarnated in the people.

This is the people's time!

Which is to say, this is humankind's time.

The hours are numbered for every enemy of humanity. As they are for imperialisms!

In the people's time, the only thing compatible with the happiness of men will be the existence of just, sovereign, and free nations, as Perón's doctrine wishes.

And that will come to pass in this century. And even if at this point it sounds like a litany of my fanaticism, it will come to pass, "whoever may fall and whatever the cost."

Imperialisms

Imperialisms…!

Perón and our people have happened upon the shame of capitalist imperialism.

I have seen its miseries and its crimes up close.

It calls itself a defender of justice as it extends its hawklike talons over the goods of all the people subjected to its omnipotence.

It proclaims itself the defender of freedom as it shackles the people who in good faith or bad must accept its unappealable demands.

Those Who Sell Out

But more abominable than imperialism are the men of national oligarchies who give up, selling or sometimes giving away the happiness of their people for coins or for smiles.

I have seen them up close, too.

Before imperialism, I have felt nothing but hateful indignation, but before those who sell out their people, to hateful indignation I have added the boundless indignation of my disdain.

I have often heard them make excuses before my sarcastic and biting aggression.

"There is nothing we can do."

I've heard that often, in every version of the lie.

A lie. Yes! A thousand lies!

There is only one invincible thing on earth: the will of the people. There are no people on earth that cannot be just, free, and sovereign.

"There is nothing we can do" is what every cowardly government of oppressed nations says.

But they do not say it out of conviction, they say it out of convenience.

By Any Means

We are a small people on the earth…and yet, with us, Perón became determined to win our own justice and our own freedom, even faced with capitalist imperialism.

And we are just and free.

The sacrifice required can vary, but it is always possible!

Nothing is stronger than the people. The only thing we have to do is decide to be just, free, and sovereign.

The process? There are a thousand effective ways to triumph: with or without arms, straight on or behind the back, by the light of day or in the shadow of night, in rage or with a smile, crying or singing, legally or by the same illicit means that imperialism itself uses against the people.

I ask myself: What can a million battleships, a million planes, and a million atom bombs do to a people determined to sabotage its masters until they attain freedom and justice?

Before wicked and despicable exploitation, everything seems small…and everything needed to triumph is important.

*

Hunger and Self-Interest

Imperialism's weapon is hunger, but our people know what it is to die of hunger.

Imperialism's Achilles' heel is its self-interest.

Where the interest of imperialism is called "oil," throwing a rock in every well will be enough to beat them.

Where it is called copper or tin, it will be enough to break the machines that extract it from the land... or for the exploited workers to fold their arms.

They cannot defeat us.

All we have to do is decide.

That is what Perón wanted from us...and we triumphed.

Now they will never be able to wrench away our justice, our freedom, our sovereignty.

They would have to kill us one by one, every Argentine.

And that...now, they can never do that.

Hate and Love

In these years of my struggle, I have learned how national and international political forces, the economic and spiritual forces of the earth, play their part in the people's government, and how they disguise the ambitions of men.

I have seen Perón, serene and unflappable, confront them, always looking beyond his life and his time, his eyes set only on the happiness of his people and the greatness of his Nation.

*

Nothing and no one could, or ever will, steer him
off his course.

I remember, in the early stage of his fight, when he
had to face the slander intended to alienate him from
his *descamisados*, claiming that he was a danger to the
people because he was from the military.

A few years later, when the slander didn't take,
his enemies tried to turn the armed forces against him,
claiming that Perón was trying to cultivate his strength
with the workers to replace the military's influence in
the Government of the Republic.

I want to tell the truth about all those things.

My authentic truth! And I hope that at some point
it prevails over so many lies…or at least—even if I am
not believed—that it is of some value to the people of
the world in their struggles for justice and freedom.

I pronounce that I belong inescapably and forever
to the "ignominious race of the people."

They will never say of me that I betrayed my
people, dazzled by the heights of power and glory. All
the rich and all the poor of my land know that.

That is why the *descamisados* love me and the others
hate and slander me.

No one in my Nation denies that for better or
worse I would not let the soul I brought from the street
be torn away from me.

That is also why—because I continue to think and
feel as part of the people—I still have not been able to
eradicate our "resentment" of the oligarchy that
exploited us.

Nor do I want to eradicate it! I say so every day
with my old indignation of a *descamisada*, harsh and

clumsy, but as sincerely as the light that cannot tell when it illuminates and when it is burning, or like the wind that cannot distinguish between clearing the clouds from the sky and sowing destruction in its path.

I do not understand middle ground or moderation.

I recognize only two words as the favored daughters of my heart: hate and love.

I never know when I hate or when I am loving.

And in this confusing encounter of hatred and love for the oligarchy of my land—and for every oligarchy in the world—I still have not been able to find the balance to reconcile myself completely with the forces among us that dared to serve the damned race of exploiters.

The High Circles

Indignant, I rebel with all the venom of my hatred or all the fire of my love—I still don't know which—against the privilege that the high circles of the armed forces and the clergy constitute.

I am well aware of what I am writing.

I know what the humble men and women that constitute the people—all the people in the world—feel and think about those circles.

I do not condemn them "personally," even though they fought and still fight me "personally" as the sworn enemy of their goals and intentions.

In the bottom of my heart, I want nothing but to save them with my accusations, showing them the road of the people, where the future of humankind lies.

I know that religion is the soul of the people; and that the people like to see the army as the powerful strength of their boys, the guarantee of their freedom, and the expression of the greatness of their Nation.

But I also know that the people are disgusted by the military dominance that monopolizes the Nation and that they cannot reconcile the humility and poverty of Christ with the pompous arrogance of the ecclesiastic dignitaries who hold an absolute monopoly on religion.

The Nation belongs to the people, just as Religion does.

I am not anti-military or anti-clergy—not in the way my enemies want to portray me.

The humble priests of the people know that. They also understand me, with the exception of a few high dignitaries of the clergy who are surrounded and blinded by the oligarchy.

The honorable in the armed forces who have not lost contact with the people know it too.

Those who refuse to understand me are the enemies of the people nestled in the military.

They refuse. They despise the people and therefore despise Perón who, as a member of the military, embraced the people's cause…even at the price of, at a certain point, abandoning his military career.

I don't see just the panorama of my own country. I see the panorama of the world, and everywhere peoples oppressed by governments that exploit their people for their own benefit or for remote, distant interests. And behind every unpopular government, I have learned to spot a military presence, underhanded and covert, or shameless and dominating.

*

In this message of my truths, I cannot silence this irrefutable truth that hovers like the darkest cloud covering the horizons of humanity.

The people must destroy the high circles of the military forces that are governing nations.

How? By opening their leading officers to the people. Armies should be of the people and should serve them...they should serve the cause of justice and liberty.

We must convince them that the Nation is not a plot of land with moveable borders; rather, it is the people...

The Nation suffers or is happy in the people that form it.

In the time of our race,....in the time of the people!...the Nation will reach its highest truth.

The armies of the world must defend their people, serving the cause of justice and freedom....Only this way will the people save themselves from falling into the hatred of "that" which was once called "the Nation...," and which was one more lie—a beautiful lie invented by the oligarchy when it began selling the people's dignity—which is to say the illustrious and wonderful dignity of the Nation!

The People, the Only Force

I don't know if the day will ever come when the world can wipe out everything that signifies a force of aggression, and the need to sustain armies in defense will therefore disappear; but until that happens—which would be the ideal, though perhaps supernatural or impossible—the people of the world must make sure

*

that the military does not turn into the chains or instruments of their own oppression.

My Nation's military monitored the elections in 1946 that established Perón as the President of the Argentines.

On that occasion, his military forces were a guarantee for the people...

In spite of that, I believe that in no case should the military function as a public guarantee of justice and freedom...because power tends to tempt men, just as money does!

The guarantee of the people's sovereign will should belong to the people. To snatch it from their hands is to acknowledge a weakness that does not exist, because the people, in ourselves, constitute the most powerful strength a nation has.

The only thing we must do is become fully aware of the power we possess and not forget that no one can do anything without the people, nor can anyone do anything the people don't want.

All the people have to do is decide that we are the masters of our own destiny!

Everything else is a matter of confronting destiny....

That is all we need to triumph!

And if not, then let our people be the ones to say so!

Serving the People

These days the world is an enormous fortress.

Every government has been dominated by the high circles of its armed forces.

Just as the Middle Ages were clerical and the Church ruled the people through the kings or the kings dominated the people by using the clergy, so in the Age of our century it is the armed forces that rule over the infiltrated people in the Governments of nations, or the Governments oppress and subjugate and exploit the people by using the colossal instrument of its armies.

Everything is military in our world. I wouldn't say a single word if the armed forces were faithful instruments of the people…but no…they are almost always the flesh of the oligarchy…why else did the oligarchy corner the high circles of the officialdom, or why else did the officials that the people gave to its armed forces sell out…forgetting the people, their pain, their immense pain!

We the people must beat the high hierarchies of the armed forces of nations.

It is not about destroying them, though I believe that at some point they will be superfluous…

It is about converting them into part of the people and then, when all of its leaders—its officials—are the flesh and spirit of the people, we will still have to remain alert, making sure they don't sell out again.

I do not believe that the solution is the one the Spartans adopted in the years of their decadence and that the generals must be elected by the people…

The people need only elect their leaders so that they do what the people want…and the generals should serve the governments of the people with clear and absolute awareness that nothing in the Nation can override or oppose the will of the people.

Greatness or Happiness

The nation is not the birthright of any force because the Nation is the people and nothing can be put above the people without jeopardizing freedom and justice.

The armed forces serve the Nation by serving the people.

The great mistake of some armed forces lies in believing that serving the Nation is something else... and then, for the sake of what they believe is the Nation, they don't mind sacrificing the people, subjecting them to the rules of military supremacy.

The same thing has happened in every century of history.

The military spirit has believed that the great ideal of its existence consists of achieving the nation's greatness and that, to reach that supreme objective, everything else was justified, including sacrificing the people's happiness.

Perón has taught us that the people's happiness comes first, that a country cannot be made great if its people are not comfortable.

The armed forces of the world should accept that absolute truth of Peronism.

If they don't,...the people themselves, with their own hands, in full consciousness of our invincible power, will erase them from the history of humankind.

We Are Stronger

All these ideas and reasons lead me to tell my people and all the people in the world this message of my truths: No one is more capable than we are.

*

We are stronger than all the armed forces of every nation put together.

If we do not want the brute force of arms to dominate us, it will not be able to dominate us.

With arms they can kill us…but dying of hunger is more painful…and we know what it is to die of hunger!

But they will not be able to kill us…. The soldiers are our sons, and even if thousands and thousands of sold-out officers beholden to the oligarchy gave them the order, they wouldn't dare open fire on their mothers.

They could defeat us in one day…at night or by surprise,…but if the next day we take to the street, or refuse to work, or sabotage everything they want to command, they will have to resign themselves to giving freedom and justice back to us.

But only if all this resistance can be better organized. If not,…we will still triumph as long as we are fully conscious of our sovereign power.

We must definitively convince ourselves of just one thing: that the government must be of the people… and no one but the people can occupy it because otherwise,…it will not be for the people either.

The hour of the people will not be achieved in our century if we do not demand active participation in the government of nations.

But how? As we have done in our country, thanks to Perón,…by placing our people's workers and women in the highest posts and responsibilities of the State. And by later making sure that the people's political leaders and the union leaders do not lose contact with the masses they represent.

The people's governors should continue to live with the people. That is a fundamental condition to ensure that the people do not start to feel betrayed and in order to govern with a real sense of what is authentically popular.

Living with the People

It is nice to live with the people. Feeling them close, suffering their pain, and rejoicing in the simple joy of their hearts.

But none of all that can be if it hasn't previously been decided to "sleep" with the people...become one body with them, so that every pain, every sorrow and worry, and all the joy of the people is as if it were ours.

That is what I did, little by little, in my life.

That is why the people make me happy and give me pain.

It makes me happy when I see them happy...and when I can add a little of my life to their happiness.

And I hurt when they suffer...I hurt when the men of the people or those who have the obligation to serve them betray the people instead of searching for their happiness.

For them, too, I also have strong and bitter words in this message of my truths.

I have seen them grow dizzy at the top.

I have seen labor leaders sell out to the owners of the oligarchy for a smile, for a banquet, or for a few coins.

And I denounce them as traitors to the enormous masses of workers—of my people and of all the people.

We must be wary of them.

They are the people's worst enemies because they have renounced our race.

They suffered with us but they forgot our pain in order to enjoy the smiling life that we gave them by granting them a trade union hierarchy.

They came to know the world of lies, of riches, of vanity, and instead of fighting them on our behalf, on behalf of our harsh and bitter truth...they sold out...

They will never come back,...but if at some point they were to come back, their foreheads should be branded with the infamous sign of treason.

The Clerical Hierarchies

Among the cold men of my era, I point out the clerical hierarchies, the vast majority of whom suffer from an inconceivable indifference before the miserable reality of the people.

I swear with absolute sincerity that these words of my pure truth hurt me like a deception.

Among the high dignitaries of the clergy, only as an exception have I seen generosity and love as the doctrine of Christ which inspired the doctrine of Perón deserve.

In them I have simply seen petty and selfish interests and a sordid ambition for privilege.

I accuse them indignantly, not for bad but for good.

I do not reproach them for having secretly conspired against Perón, in their conciliabules with the oligarchy.

I do not reproach them for having been ungrateful to Perón, who gave them his Christian heart as well as his good will and his faith.

I reproach them for having abandoned the poor, the humble, the *descamisados*, the sick...and for having preferred, instead, the glory and the honors of the oligarchy.

I reproach them for having betrayed Christ, who was compassionate with the masses..., forgetting the people. And I reproach them for having done everything possible to hide the name and the figure of Christ behind the curtain of smoke with which they flatter it.

I am and I feel Christian...because I am Catholic,... but I do not understand how Christ's religion can be compatible with the oligarchy and privilege.

I will never understand this. As the people do not understand it.

If they wish to save the world from spiritual destruction, the clergy in the new era must convert to Christianity, beginning by coming down to the people...as Christ did, suffering with the people,... feeling with the people.

Because they do not live or suffer or feel or think with the people. The years of Perón are passing over their hearts without inspiring a single resonance....

Their hearts are closed and cold.

Oh, if they knew how beautiful the people are,... they would jump to defend them for Christ, who today, as he did two thousand years ago, has compassion for the masses.

Religion

Christ asked them to evangelize the poor,...and that is why they should never abandon the people, where the immense masses of poor are.

Politicians of the church throughout every era and in every country have wanted to exercise dominion over and even exploit the people through the Church and Religion. And very often, to the disgrace of faith, the clergy has served the politicians who are the people's enemies, preaching a stupid resignation—which I still do not know how they reconcile with human dignity or with the thirst for Justice whose blessedness is sung in the Gospel.

The clerical politician also attempts in every country to exercise dominion over and even to exploit the people through the government, and this, too, endangers the people's happiness.

Both paths of political clericalism and clerical politics should be avoided by the people of the world if they want to be happy one day.

I do not believe as Lenin did that religion is the opium of the people.

Instead, religion should be the liberation of the people; because when man meets God he reaches the heights of his extraordinary dignity.

If God did not exist, if we were not destined for God, if there were no religion, man would be a few specks of dust scattered into the abyss of eternity.

But God does exist, and to him we are worthy and to him we are all equal and before him no one has privilege over anyone.

*

We are all equal!

I do not understand, therefore, how, in the name of Religion and in the name of God, resignation before injustice can be preached...and why, instead, in the name of God and in the name of Religion, those supreme rights of all—to justice and liberty—cannot be reclaimed.

Religion should never be an instrument of oppression for the people.

It has to be a banner of rebellion.

Religion is in the people's soul because the people live close to God, in touch with the pure air of his immensity.

No one can stop the people from having faith.

If they were to lose it, all of humanity would be lost forever.

I rebel against the "religions" that make men bow their heads and people bow their souls.

That cannot be religion.

Religion should lift the heads of men.

I admire the religion that can make an emperor say to a humble *descamisado*, "I am the same as you, son of God!"

Religion will regain its prestige among the people if its preachers teach it that way...as a force of rebellion and equality, not as an instrument of oppression.

To preach resignation is to preach slavery.

Instead, we must preach liberty and justice.

Love is the only path by which religion will live to see the day of the people.

＊

Forms and Principles

I live with my heart clinging to my people's heart and I therefore know every time their heart beats. I know how they feel, how they think, and how they suffer.

It doesn't escape me that I have often been duped and that in religious matters, the people have too many prejudices and they accept numerous mistakes.

I do not feel authorized to judge this transcendental subject. My message is destined to awaken the soul of the people from their sleepy ignorance of the infinite forms of oppression.

And one of those forms is the one that uses our people's profound religious conviction as an instrument of slavery.

Religious conviction should be defended by the people, and all its perversions therefore deserve unpardonable condemnation.

I believe that those who believe that religion is a simple set of external formalities have done as much evil to humanity as have those who see nothing but absolutely rigid principles.

Religion is for man and not man for religion, and therefore religion should be profoundly human,... profoundly popular!

And for religion to be so—profoundly popular— it must return to what it was before.

It should speak again in the language of the heart, which is the language of the people, forgetting the excessive rituals and the likewise excessive theological complications.

*

When you speak simply and lovingly to the people, the people comprehend the truth offered them. And all the more faithfully if it is preached by example.

Unfortunately, our people and perhaps all the people on earth have seen only too much self-interest in the preachers of the faith,...and that may be precisely why they have closed their hearts to them!

The People and God

Many times, in these years of my life, I have thought about how far away certain preachers and apostles of religion are from the heart of the people,...because the coldness and selfishness of their souls could not infect anyone or sow in anyone's soul the fervor of the faith— which is a passionate fire.

I know—and I declare it with all the strength of my spirit—that the people thirst for God.

And I also know how the humble priests work to quench that thirst.

My accusation is aimed not at them but rather at those who out of selfishness, vanity, pride, self-interest, or any other reason disgrace the cause they claim to defend, separating the people from the truth, closing off the path to God for them.

Some day, God will exact from them the precise cost of their betrayal,...much more severely than from those of us who, with less theology but more love, decided to give everything for the people...with all our souls, with all our hearts!

*

The Ambitious

The ambitious are also enemies of the people.

I have often seen them come up to Perón, first as gentle and loyal friends fooling even me, proclaiming a loyalty that later I would have to retract.

The ambitious are cold like snakes, but they know how to dissemble all too well.

They are the people's enemies because they will never serve the people, but only their personal interests.

I have persecuted them within the Peronist movement, and I will continue to persecute them relentlessly in defense of the people.

They are the *caudillos*.

Their souls are closed to all that is not them.

They do not work for a doctrine, nor do they care about an ideal.

The doctrine and the ideal are themselves.

The people's time will not come with any *caudillo* because *caudillos* die, and the people are eternal.

That is why Perón is great—because he has no ambition other than the happiness of his people and the greatness of his Nation. And because he has created a doctrine—a doctrine is an ideal—for his people to follow his doctrine and not his name.

But I believe that when the people find a man who is worthy of them, they do not follow his doctrine, but rather his name, because in the man and in the name they see the doctrine itself personified; and they cannot conceive of the doctrine without its creator.

*

That is why I cannot conceive of Justicialism without Perón; and that is why I have so often pronounced myself a Peronist as opposed to a justicialist, because justicialism is the doctrine. Peronism, on the other hand, is Perón *and* the doctrine…the living reality that has made us and makes us happy!

Caudillos, on the other hand, the ambitious, do not have a doctrine because they have no motive other than their selfishness.

We must seek them out and brand them with an iron so that they never become the masters of the people's lives and property.

I have known them up close and personal; and at times they have fooled even me, at least temporarily.

They must be identified. They must be destroyed. The people's cause exclusively requires men of the people who work for the people, not for themselves.

This is where the ambitious can be discerned, in that they work for themselves, for nothing but themselves.

They never seek the happiness of the people; rather, they always seek their own vanity and to get rich quick.

Money, power, and honors are the three great "causes," the three "ideals" of all ambitious men.

I have never met an ambitious man who was not pursuing one of these three things—or all three at once.

The people have to be careful about the men they elect to manage their destinies. And they must reject and destroy them when they see them thirsting for wealth, power, or honors.

*

The thirst for wealth is easy to spot. It is the first to appear, apparent to all.

Union leaders above all must be watched over.

They, too, grow dizzy. It must not be forgotten that when a politician allows himself to be dominated by ambition, he is nothing more than an ambitious man, but when a union leader gives in to the desire for money or power or honors, he is a traitor and deserves to be punished as a traitor.

Power and honor also intensely seduce men and create ambitious men. They start working for themselves and they forget the people.

This is the only way to identify them...and the people have to recognize and destroy them.

Only this way will the people be free, because every ambitious man is a dictator capable of becoming a tyrant.

We must watch out for them like we would the devil!

~

I don't want to die because of Perón and because of my *descamisados*.

Not for myself, as I have already lived all that I had to live.

Perón and the poor need me.

~

Will my "*grasitas*"* know how much I loved them?

* A slang term of endearment for the lowest members of the lower class. Trans.

＊

~

If someone were to ask me, in this difficult and bitter period of my life, what my most fervent desire is and what my deepest wish is, I would tell him this: to live with Perón and with my people forever.

Many times, in the long and harsh hours of my illness, I have wanted to live, not for myself—for I have already received everything I could ask for from life and still more—but for Perón and for my "*grasitas*," for my *descamisados*.

Sickness and pain have brought me close to God, and I have realized that everything that is happening to me and all that is making me suffer is not unfair.

When I married Perón, I had every opportunity to take the wrong path that leads to the headiness of high places.

Instead, God took me down my people's roads and because I followed them, I have come to receive the affection of men, women, children, and the elderly as no one else has.

But I do ask God for a little vacation from my suffering.

The Great Crime

Many times, especially during the years of the revolution, I would hear the high military officials trying to dissuade the "Colonel" from his love of the people.

They could not comprehend how a superior officer could "give in" that way to the "riffraff."

At first they thought the Colonel was practicing demagoguery to attain power.

It was then that, envious of Perón's success, they started the first revolution, they demanded the Colonel's resignation, and they jailed him in Martín García.

But happily, the people had already come to know Perón. They no longer saw him as the military chief with the calling of a dictator but rather as the colleague whose heart had felt the pain of our race.

And the people took to the streets, ready for anything. The reactionist military chiefs fled in fear, and the oligarchy hid with them.

That was October 17, 1945.

Later, things changed.

The Colonel, now President, remained loyal to his *descamisados*.

Now it was impossible for him to be a demagogue as they claimed.

The fact that Perón, a military chief, was conceding fundamental importance to the workers of his people was confirmed.

And as the workers started organizing, becoming the most powerful force in the country, the oligarchy, who had also infiltrated the armed forces, was preparing the resistance.

I have witnessed Perón's harsh battle with the privilege of the armed forces, as harsh as the fights against the privilege of money or of blood.

I know how he has suffered even though I have had the rare and marvelous privilege of being something like the shield on which the attacks of his enemies always shattered.

Cowardly, like all traitors, they never attacked him straight on, they attacked him through me. I was the great pretext!

I carried out my duty, joyful and happy, blocking the shots that were aimed at Perón.

However, those who didn't like me always ended up distancing themselves from Perón. In one way or another, they left. And many betrayed him!

The truth, the real and pure truth, is that the great majority of those who did not like Perón because of me didn't like him without me either.

The people, on the other hand, the *descamisados*, the workers, the women, who love me more than I deserve, are Perón fanatics to the death.

Perón's strength resides with the people, not with the army. Only the people love Perón fanatically and sincerely. And when several officers of the armed forces recently tried to "terminate" Perón, they found themselves having to confront the people, who surrounded their Leader and, without protection, opposed the traitors. The infinite strength of the heart.

Even in the army, the loyal men, including those who fell in defense of Perón, were men of the people, humble but noble and loyal in the face of the treasonous defection of the oligarchy.

That day, the 28th of September, I was profoundly pleased to have renounced the vice presidency of the Republic on August 22nd and 31st.

If I hadn't, I would have been the great pretext once again.

Instead, the revolution ended up proving that the military reaction was against Perón..., against the vile crime committed by Perón of "giving in" to the will of the people, fighting and working for the happiness of the poor against the dominance and the collusion of all the privileged with all the forces of the unpatriotic.

This is Perón's great crime!

The great crime that I bless from the bottom of my *descamisado* heart.

In me, all the love and affection I feel for my people are not important and have no value because I came from the people, I suffered with the people.

By contrast, Perón's love for the *descamisados* is worth infinitely more,…because given his rank as Colonel, the easiest path of his life would have been that of the oligarchy and its privileges.

Instead, he sided with the people, against all odds, overcoming the resistance of many of his peers, and he embraced our cause wholeheartedly.

He committed the great crime!

I believe that in committing it, he alone saved my Nation's armed forces from discredit and dishonor, for if Perón had not been of the military, our people would have been convinced that the armed forces were a redoubt of the oligarchy.

In this year of Perón, the military has the great opportunity to secure a future for itself,…helping Perón in this work of "serving the people," working from the fundamental base that that is not a crime, because it is serving the Nation.

✳

My Supreme Will

I want to live with Perón and with my People forever.

This is my absolute and final wish, and it will therefore also be, when my time is up, the last wish of my heart.

Wherever Perón is, and wherever my *descamisados* are, there, too, will be my heart to love them with all the strength of my life and with all the fanaticism of my soul.

If God were to take Perón from the world before me, I would go with him, because I would not be able to survive without him. But my heart would remain with my *descamisados*, with my women, my workers, my elderly, my children, to help them live with the affection of my love; to help them fight with the fire of my fanaticism; and to help them suffer with a little of my own pain.

Because I have suffered greatly; but my pain has been worth the people's happiness,…and I did not want to deny it—I do not want to deny it—I accept suffering to the last day of my life if that will serve to stop the bleeding of even one wound, or dry even one tear.

But if God were to take me from the world before Perón, I want to remain with him and with my people, and my heart and my affection and my soul and my fanaticism will stay with them. Those things will keep living in them, doing all the good that is lacking, giving them all the love I couldn't give them in the years of my life, and lighting the fire of my fanaticism that burns and consumes me like a bitter and infinite thirst in their souls every day.

I will be with them so that they continue down the open road of justice and freedom until the wonderful day of the people arrives.

I will be with them fighting against everything that is not pure people, against everything that is not the "ignominious" race of the people.

I will be with them, with Perón and with my people, to fight against the country-selling and charlatan oligarchy, against the cursed race of exploiters and merchants of the people.

God is the witness to my sincerity, and he knows that the love for my race—which is the people— consumes me.

Everything that opposes the people outrages me to the extreme limits of my rebelliousness and my hatred.

But God also knows that I have never hated anyone for themselves, nor have I fought anyone mean-spiritedly. I have fought, but rather, to defend my people, my workers, my women, my poor *"grasitas"* whom no one ever defended with more sincerity than Perón or with more fervor than "Evita."

But Perón's love for the people is greater than mine, because he, from his military privilege, knew how to connect with the people, he knew how to climb up to the people, breaking all the chains of his caste. I, on the other hand, was born with the people and suffered with the people. I have the flesh and spirit and blood of the people. I could do no other thing than devote myself to my people.

If I were to die before Perón, I would want this will of mine, the last and definitive of my life, to be read in a public ceremony in the Plaza de Mayo, in the Plaza del 17 de octubre, before my beloved *descamisados.*

I want them to know, at that moment, that I loved and I love Perón with all my soul and that Perón is my son and sky. God will not let me lie if I repeat at that moment one more time, like Leon Bloy, that "I cannot imagine the sky without Perón."

I beg all the workers, all the poor, all the *descamisados*, all the women, all the kids, and all the elderly of my Nation to take care of him and keep him company as if they were me.

I want all of my possessions left at Perón's disposal as the sovereign and only representative of the people.

I desire that all my possessions, which, to a large extent, I consider the inheritance of the people and of the Peronist movement—which is of the people —and that all that *My Reason for Being* and "My Message" earn be considered the property of Perón and the Argentine people.

For as long as Perón lives, he may do what he wishes with my belongings: sell them, donate them, even burn them if he wishes, because everything in my life belongs to him, everything is his, beginning with my very life, which I gave to him absolutely out of love and forever.

But after Perón, the only heir to my belongings must be the people, and I beg the workers and the women of my people to demand, by any means, the inexorable fulfillment of this supreme will of my heart that loved them so much.

All the possessions I have mentioned and even those I may have omitted should serve the people, in one way or another.

The money from *My Reason for Being* and "My Message," just like the sale or proceeds from my belongings, should be marked for my *descamisados*.

With all those belongings, I would like to set up a permanent fund of social aid for cases of collective misfortune that affect the poor, and I would like them to accept it as one more proof of my affection.

In those cases, for example, I want a subsidy equal to at least one year's salary granted to each family.

With that permanent "Evita" fund, I also want to establish scholarships so that the workers' children can study and thereby become the defenders of Perón's doctrine for whose delightful cause I would give my life.

My jewelry does not belong to me. Most of it was gifts from my people. But even what I received from my friends or from foreign countries, or from the General, I want to return to the people.

I never want it to fall into the hands of the oligarchy, and that's why I want it to constitute in the museum of Peronism, a permanent credit to be used only in direct benefit to the people.

Just as in some countries money is backed by gold, my jewelry should be the backing of a permanent credit that the national Banks will open for the benefit of the people, with the goal of building housing for the workers of my Nation.

I would also wish that the poor, the elderly, the children, my *descamisados* would continue to write me as they do in these times of my life, and that the monument which the Congress of my People wanted to erect for me* would reflect the hopes of all, and that those hopes would be made real through my Foundation; which I hope will always remain pure, the way I conceived it for my *descamisados*.

*Evita's final resting place was to have been part of a gigantic monument to be constructed in downtown Buenos Aires. The military coup that overthrew Perón in 1955 caused the project to be aborted. Trans.

This way I will always feel close to my people, and I will continue to be the bridge of love drawn between the *descamisados* and Perón.

Finally, I want everyone to know that if I made mistakes, I made them out of love. I hope that God, who has always seen my heart, will judge me not by my mistakes or my defects or my faults, which are many, but rather by the love that consumes my life.

My last words are the same as the first. I want to live with Perón and with my People forever.

God will forgive me if I would rather stay with them because he, too, is with the poor, and I have always seen a little bit of God in every *descamisado* who asked me for a little love, which I never withheld.

One Single Class

The men and women of the people must always be partisan and fanatics; they must never give in to the oligarchy.

As Perón's doctrine states, there can never be more than one single class: those who work.

The people must impose this Peronist truth on the entire world.

The union leaders and the women, who are pure people, cannot, must not, give in to the oligarchy.

I am not making an issue of class. I am not patronizing the class struggle, but our dilemma is very clear.

The oligarchy that exploited us for thousands of years throughout the world will always try to defeat us.

*

But we will never reach an understanding with them because the one thing they want is the one thing we will never give them: our freedom.

To avoid a class struggle, I do not believe, as the Communists do, that we must kill all the oligarchs of the world. No. Because that would be a never-ending thing, for once the current ones disappeared, we would have to start with our men who turned into oligarchy in the name of ambition, honors, money, or power.

The path is to convert all the oligarchs of the world and turn them into the people,... of our class and of our race.

How? By making them work in order to join the only class that Perón recognizes: the class of men who work.

Work is the great task of men, but it is the great virtue.

When everyone works, when everyone lives off their own work and not off someone else's, we will all be better, more brotherly; and the oligarchy will be a bitter and painful memory for humankind.

But meanwhile, it is essential that the men of the people, of the working class, not sell out to the oligarchic race of exploiters.

Every exploiter is the people's enemy.

Justice demands that they be destroyed!

FACSIMILES OF PAGES
FROM THE RECOVERED MANUSCRIPT
OF *MI MENSAJE.*
(E. P. STANDS FOR EVA PERÓN.)

Eva Perón

16 Servir al pueblo

En estos momentos el mundo es una inmensa fortaleza.

Todos los Gobiernos han sido dominados por los altos círculos de sus fuerzas armadas.

Así como la Edad Media fué clerical y la Iglesia gobernó sobre los pueblos por medio de los reyes o los reyes dominaron a los pueblos valiéndose del clero así en la Edad de nuestro siglo las fuerzas armadas mandan sobre los pueblos infiltradas en los Gobiernos de las naciones o los Gobiernos oprimen y sojuzgan y explotan a los pueblos. valiéndose del instrumento colosal dd sus ejércitos.

Todo es militar en este mundo nuestro. Yo no diría una sola palabra si las fuerzas armadas fuesen instrumentos fieles del pueblo... pero no... son casi siempre carne de oligarquía... o porque la oligarquía copó los altos círculos de la oficialidad o porque los oficiales que el pueblo dió a sus fuerzas armadas se entregaron... olvidándose del pueblo, de sus dolores, ! de su inmenso dolor!

Eva Perón

Nosotros, el pueblo tenemos que ganar las altas
jerarquías de las fuerzas militares, aéreas y nave
les de las naciones. *armadas*

No se trata de destruirlas, aunque yo pienzo que
alguna vez serán inútiles...

Se trata de convertirlas al pueblo y después,
cuando todos sus dirigentes - sus oficiales - sean
carne y alma del pueblo habrá que permanecer alertas,
vigilándolas para que no se entreguen otra vez...

Yo no creo que la solución sea la que adoptaron
los espartanos en los años de su decadencia y que los
generales tengan que ser elegidos por el pueblo...

El pueblo sólo tiene que elegir a sus gobernantes
para que ellos hagan lo que el pueblo quiere... y los
generales deben servir al gobierno del pueblo con ple
na y absoluta conciencia de que nada en la Nación pue
de sobreponerse ni oponerse a la voluntad del pueblo.

 - - - o - - -

Eva Perón

17 La grandeza o la felicidad

La Patria no es patrimonio de ninguna fuerza
porque la Patria es el pueblo y nada puede sobreponerse al pueblo sin que corran peligro la libertad
y la justicia.

Las fuerzas armadas sirven a la Patria sirviendo
al pueblo.

El gran error de las/ algunas fuerzas armadas consiste en
creer que servir a la Patria es una cosa distinta...
y entonces en aras de lo que ellos creen que es la
Patria no les importa sacrificar al pueblo, sometién
dolo a las reglas de la prepotencia militar.

En todos los siglos de la historia ha sucedido lo
mismo.

El espíritu militar ha considerado que el gran
ideal de su existencia consistía en alcanzar la gran
deza de la nación y que, ante ese objetivo supremo
se justificaba todo, incluso sacrificar la felicidad
del pueblo.

Perón nos ha enseñado que la felicidad del pueblo

Eva Perón

es lo primero· que no se puede hacer la grandeza de
un país con un pueblo que no tiene bienestar.

Las fuerzas armadas del mundo deben convencerse
de esta absoluta verdad del peronismo.

Si no... los pueblos mismos, por su propia mano,
con la conciencia plena de nuestro poderío insupera
ble, las iremos borrando en la historia de la huma-
nidad.

- - - o - - - *E.P.*

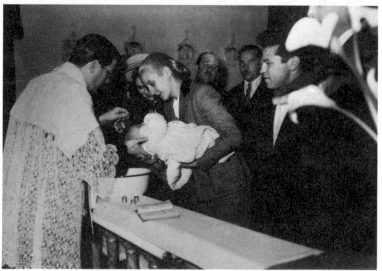

VIDA ARTISTICA DE

EVA DUARTE

90 FOTOS PROHIBIDAS

POR LA
DICTADURA

Vemos al costado a Eva y
Samuel Yankelevich en plena danza durante una fiesta
ofrecida a la dama por el
padre del nombrado Abajo
aparece la "gran actriz" en
compañía del galan Aldo
Fertierista que luce un im-
pecable bisoñé.

LUCIENDO CREACIONES

Vemos en esta página a Eva Duarte
luciendo diversas creaciones en el
año 1942, época en que era modelo
de una casá de modas.

NO LEA

LEA LO MEJOR,
Y LO MEJOR ES
EN HUMORISMO ES
EL REPORTER

CACHADITAS

(Ex POCHOLANDIA)

que le ofrece los más sabrosos
chistes de carácter general y las
más finas cachaditas políticas.

VIDA ARTISTICA
de
EVA DUARTE

$ 3.—

90 FOTOS
PROHIBIDAS
POR LA DICTADURA

EL REPORTER *CACHARRAS*
Edición Especial

A CONVERSATION WITH
JUAN JIMÉNEZ DOMÍNGUEZ

BY ALBERTO SCHPREJER*

*J*UAN JIMÉNEZ DOMÍNGUEZ was probably the most eminent of the aides to whom, in the final months of her life, Evita dictated "My Message." Jiménez is in his seventies, a thin and elegant man who, in a serious and confident voice, boasts of having served the "Señora" diligently and loyally.

He admits that he considered the book lost forever. "The military," he explains, "destroyed almost everything that had belonged to Eva Perón, whom they hated viscerally."

He says he learned that that might not be the case a few years ago when a few "people from the Guardia de Hierro," an internal organization of officers of the Justicialist movement, paid him a visit. They inquired about the document's authenticity.

"I asked them for a copy of the original in order to authenticate it with complete certainty, but they never came back," he says.

If he was so sure he could render an opinion about the authenticity of the original, he added, it is because "I typed many of those pages myself, and even though I never had all of the pages together in one place, almost every page passed through my hands....If I didn't type every page it was because I was on assignments outside Buenos Aires and because Evita dictated them in her spare moments to whichever aide was closest at hand."

Even though the people from Guardia de Hierro never returned to consult with him, he adds, "I understand that they were involved in the purchase of the manuscript. "He says that

* Alberto Schprejer is the Argentine publisher of a 1994 edition of *Mi mensaje*. This interview was conducted in 1992 for that edition. We are grateful to Schprejer for his permission to reprint it here.

the document's ranting and emotional style comes from the fact that Evita "had a fantastic intuition and a great facility with words. She loved to improvise, to say what sprang from her heart and, in fact, she rarely re-read her work."

Jiménez first met Eva on the eve of October 17, 1945, and from 1948 until her death was one of her closest collaborators. He knew her before Peronism was firmly established and before she married Perón. He met her during the feverish days in which Evita was urging the union delegates to organize the uprising that would liberate then Colonel Perón from his confinement on the island of Martín García.

Jiménez recalls the date of October 8, 1945 (the date that Perón turned 50 years old and the date that the oligarchy's armed forces detained Perón and took him to the island), when Evita convened a meeting of unionized workers, where she vehemently called for them to organize an active strike, which, in fact, took place nine days later.

One of the people there who caught Evita's attention for his youthfulness turned out to be Jiménez. At the time he was a twenty-three-year-old teacher determined to form the first teacher's union, a union that was founded shortly thereafter under the name of Unión de Docentes Argentinos (UDA), and of which Jiménez would be the first secretary general.

From then on, Jiménez was in direct contact with Eva, a relationship that was formalized when, "in 1948 she invited me to come work in her office in the Department of Labor and Welfare."

Forty-four years have gone by, but Jiménez remembers it as if it were yesterday. "From that moment on, I became the Señora's close and constant collaborator."

Jiménez lays out four old photographs that show him next to Evita and Perón. He says that at his boss's side, working fourteen- and fifteen-hour days, he realized the magnitude of her profoundly humane and Christian work. As for Evita's ill will toward bishops and cardinals, Jiménez says that "Evita was very Christian, very Catholic, you could even say militant, and she always made confession to Father Hernán Benítez. So if she did not get along well with the clergy, it was simply because they systematically sided with the oligarchy. The proof of what I'm telling you is that in every construction the Foundation ever built, there was always a chapel."

With respect to her acute distrust of generals, he says that the military "had profound respect for Evita because they knew that anything that reached her ears, she immediately passed on to Perón. I believe," he continues, "that the 1955 coup did not occur earlier only because of Evita's presence. She was an absolute buffer: she always stood by the worker's movement and one word from her could launch a general strike the same day. And everyone complied with the unions' decisions because almost every worker was a Peronist."

He speaks of Eva's illness, the illness that those who hated her welcomed joyfully to the point of shouting "*Long live cancer!*"

"She refused medical treatment because she said that the most important thing was to continue working for the poor, that she could not afford the luxury of checking into a hospital or, by indulging her ill health, neglect those who were suffering more," he recalls. "Finally, she had no choice but to check into a hospital. I think it was November 6 or 7, 1951. I was in Mar del Plata at the time and she instructed me to call her every day to update her on my work. The municipal elections were held on November 11, 1951, and for the first time Peronism won. I remember calling the hospital around midnight because Eva was extremely interested in the results and had insisted that I call no matter what time.

"I also remember with particular emotion that a few days after her health had improved a little and she had moved back into the residence on Austria Street (which the guerrillas later demolished), Evita's private secretary, Renzi, called me and asked me to come over. When I arrived, I was led to her room.

"She was in an armchair, wearing a pink nightgown; she was as pale as a lily, but beautiful," he says and chokes on his voice.

Clearly, the scene is fixed in his memory, an even more indelible image than those in the pile of real photographs picturing him next to his boss.

"It was almost noon. I kissed her as I always did and she asked me to take a seat. I sat there for twenty minutes and, since she didn't utter a word, I finally said '*Señora, you called for me, I am at your service, anything.*'"

Jiménez's eyes well up behind his glasses. He hesitates for a moment, and swallows in order to continue.

"Then she reached out her hand, her left hand. She touched me on the shoulder and said: '*No, Jiménez, I called for you only because I needed to be with a true Peronist.*' Then she fell silent again, and after two or three minutes she added, '*Go, the General is coming and he still doesn't want me to talk to anyone.*'"

Questioned if at any time he spoke to Evita about the contents of "My Message" and the repercussions its publication might have, Jiménez says no.

"We didn't have to because I completely agreed with what she was dictating. Don't forget that I was more Evita's man than Perón's. Don't forget that day after day I saw her devotion to her redeeming work, I witnessed how she attended the poor and the workers." He pauses then states: "She was full of tenderness. She was a blessing for Argentina."

CHRONOLOGY

OF EVA PERÓN'S LIFE

1919, MAY 7. In Colonia Agrícola La Unión, near the town of Los Toldos, Eva María Duarte, the daughter of don Juan Duarte and doña Juana Ibarguren is born.
NOVEMBER 21. She is baptized in the Church of Nuestra Señora Pilar.

1924, JANUARY 8. Her father dies in an accident.

1927-29. Eva is enrolled in grade school in Los Toldos.

1930-33. She completes her studies in Junín, where her family has moved.

EARLY 1934. In Buenos Aires, Eva's brother Juan enlists in the military service.

1935, JANUARY. At age fifteen, Evita comes to Argentina's capitol, Buenos Aires.
MARCH 28. She lands her first theater role in Eva Franco's company. Her debut is in Ernesto Marsili's comedy, *La señora de Perez*.
JUNE 19. Her second theater role, in *Cada casa es un mundo* by Goicoechea

and Cordone, is performed on the same stage.
NOVEMBER 26. The comedy *Madame Sans Gêne* by Moreau and Sardou opens in the Cómico Theater. In it, Evita plays a more important role, next to Eva Franco.

1936, JANUARY 2. Eva plays the role of the typist in the play *La dama, el caballero y el ladrón* by Federico Mateos Vidal in the Cómico Theater.
JUNE-AUGUST. She tours throughout Argentina with José Franco's company.
DECEMBER 5. Lilian Hellman's *Las inocentes (The Children's Hour)* opens in the Corrientes Theater. Eva plays the role of a Latin student.

1937, MARCH 5. She appears in *La nueva colonia* by Pirandello, directed by Armando Discépolo.
Evita is cast in her first film role, *Segundos afuera* directed by Chas de Cruz.
AUGUST. Eva lands her first job in radio theater, *Oro blanco (White Cold)* by Manuel Ferrandás Campos.
NOVEMBER 5. Eva has a role in *No hay suegra como la mía* by Marcos Bronenberg at the Liceo Theater.

1938. Eva works in the theater with Pierini Dealessi, Marcos Zucker, and

Pascual Pelliciotta. She also works in radio theater.

1939. She has roles in Camila Quirogas's company.
MAY 1. She is the featured actress of the radio theater company performing *Los jazmines del ochenta* by Héctor Pedro Blomberg.
MAY 20. She is featured on the cover of *Antena* magazine.

1940, JUNE 12. *La Carga de los valientes*, a film by Adelqui Millar in which Eva has a role, has its premiere.

1941, MARCH 19. Premiere of the movie *El más infeliz del pueblo* by Luis Bayon Herrera, in which Eva plays a provincial teenager.
MARCH 27. Eva appears on the cover of the magazine *Cine Argentino*.
OCTOBER. She is the understudy in the film *Una novia en apuros* directed by North American John Reinhardt and released the following year.

1942, MARCH. She works in a radio theater company.
JUNE 10. *Sintonía* magazine publishes an article about Evita Duarte titled *El encanto del perfume en la mujer* (*The Charm of the Scent of a Woman*). She continues her work in radio.

1943, AUGUST 3. The Asociación Radial Argentina (Association of Argentine Radio) is founded. Eva is the spokesperson.
OCTOBER 16. She returns to radio (after months without work)

performing biographies of celebrated women in history.

1944, JANUARY 19-22. The first encounters take place between Evita Duarte and Colonel Juan Perón.
FEBRUARY 3. Over Radio Belgrano, her company broadcasts the life of Carlota of Mexico.
APRIL. The life of Sara Bernhardt is broadcast.
MAY. The life of Alejandra Feodorovna is broadcast. In the second half of the month, the shooting of *La Cabalgata del circo* begins (*Circus Cavalcade*). In the film, she works with Hugo del Carril and Libertad Lamarque.
JUNE 3. She is on the cover of the magazine *Radiolandia*. She begins the program *Hacia un Futuro Mejor* (*Toward a Better Future*) written by Francisco J. Azpiri. She also continues her series of historical heroines.

1945, APRIL. She has a leading role in the film *La pródiga* (*The Gorgeous Woman*) under the direction of Mario Soffici.
MAY 1. She is on the cover of *Sintonía*.
MAY 31. *La cabalgata del circo* premieres.
OCTOBER 13. She is separated from Colonel Perón when he is taken to the island of Martín García.
OCTOBER 18. A joyful reunion with Perón upon his release.
OCTOBER 22. In a civil ceremony in Junín, she marries the Colonel, becoming María Eva Duarte de Perón.
DECEMBER 10. Religious wedding in the Church of San Francisco in the city of La Plata.

CHRONOLOGY

DECEMBER 31. She waits for Perón in Santiago del Estero, during the first tour of the presidential candidate.

1946, FEBRUARY. She accompanies Perón on his campaign tours to the country's interior.

MAY 1. She marches down the streets of Buenos Aires at the newly elected President's side.

LATE MAY. She pays her first visits to manufacturing plants.

JUNE. She moves into an office in the Palacio del Correo with the help of Oscar Nicolini. There, she starts meeting with union delegates to address their issues.

JULY 5. She initiates a campaign on behalf of the poor children in Argentina's interior.

AUGUST 2. She is named Best Samaritan by the Asociación del Personal de Hospitales y Sanatorios Particulares (Association of Hospital and Private Sanatorium Personnel). She cannot attend because she is ill.

LATE AUGUST. She is struck by a new illness.

SEPTEMBER 11. She re-emerges at the Chamber of Deputies to expedite the passage of a bill promoting civic rights for women. She now works out of an office in the Department of Labor and Welfare.

OCTOBER-NOVEMBER. She visits Córdoba, Berisso, and Tucumán.

1947, JANUARY 27. She delivers a radio message about the future vote for women.

MARCH 12. She gives another speech about women's rights.

APRIL 14. She calls together the women of America on the Day of the Americas.

MAY 31. She receives an honorary degree from the University of La Plata.

JUNE 3. She inaugurates the first temporary housing units in Buenos Aires.

JUNE 6. She departs for Spain on her "Rainbow" tour of Europe, representing the president.

JUNE 9. She receives the Cross of Isabel the Catholic from Spain's Generalíssimo Franco. A crowd applauds her from Madrid's Plaza de Oriente.

JULY 21. She arrives in Paris.

JUNE 27. She meets with Pope Pius XII in the Vatican.

JULY 27-30. She visits Portugal.

AUGUST 3. By train, she travels to Geneva.

AUGUST 16. She flies to Rio de Janeiro.

AUGUST 21. In Montevideo, Uruguay, she meets with President Batile Berres.

AUGUST 23. A crowd welcomes her home in the Northern Port of Buenos Aires.

SEPTEMBER 8. After a brief illness, she resumes her activities in the Department of Labor and Welfare.

SEPTEMBER 9. Women's civic rights are sanctioned with Evita present in the Congress.

SEPTEMBER 23. She delivers a speech in Buenos Aires's Plaza de Mayo during the ceremony enacting Law Number 13,010, which gave women the right to vote in Argentina.

OCTOBER 23. In Sanandita, Bolivia, she receives the *Gran cruz del cóndor* of the Andes, from President Enrique G. Hertzog.

117

OCTOBER 26. In the town of Resistencia, in the province of El Chaco, she addresses textile factory workers.

OCTOBER 28. She meets with President Higinio Morínigo of Paraguay, who decorates her with the *Gran cruz.*

1948, APRIL 3. She announces the construction of *Ciudad Evita*, capital of the province of Buenos Aires during the Peronist regime.

MAY 12. She inaugurates a library that she donated to the Confederación General del Trabajo (CGT), the syndicate of trade unions.

MAY 16. She travels to Santiago del Estero with 150 of the children whom the *Fundacion de Ayuda Social María Eva Duarte de Perón* (María Eva Duarte de Perón Foundation for Social Aid) is educating.

JUNE 19. Eva is present at the opening of the second *Hogar del Tránsito* (shelter) in Buenos Aires. This same day the Foundation is formally established.

JULY 21. An article by Eva titled "Why I Am a Peronist" appears in the newspaper *Democracia.*

AUGUST 14. The inauguration of the third *Hogar del Tránsito.*

AUGUST 28. She announces the Decalog of Rights for Senior Citizens, which is translated into five languages.

OCTOBER 17. She inaugurates the Colonel Perón Home for the Elderly in Burzaco.

OCTOBER 27. Her article "The Argentine Woman Supports Reform" appears in *Democracia.*

NOVEMBER 27-30. She travels to Mendoza and Córdoba to promote constitutional reform.

1949, JULY 14. Eva and Juan inaugurate the Amanda Allen Orphanage.

JULY 30. Eva is named President of the Peronist Feminist Party.

SEPTEMBER 5. The Foundation airlifts aid to the victims of an earthquake in Equador.

1950, JANUARY 9. Eva suffers a breakdown at the ceremony inaugurating the headquarters of the Taxi Driver's Union.

JANUARY 12. Dr. Oscar Ivanessevich performs an appendectomy and detects cancer.

JANUARY 27. Eva resumes her work in the Department of Labor and Welfare.

MARCH 8. She suspends her work due to health problems.

APRIL 9. She rests with Perón in the resort town of Bariloche.

MAY 1. She delivers a speech emphasizing her role as a "bridge of love" between Perón and the people.

JUNE 10. She inaugurates two manufacturing schools in Buenos Aires.

JULY 3. She oversees the distribution of the first 1,000 pensions to the elderly.

SEPTEMBER 1. The Eva Perón Circle, a group of young writers loyal to the Peronist regime who gathered together once a week to share their work, is officially founded in the Women Workers' Home.

SEPTEMBER 4. The María Eva Duarte de Perón School of Nurses joins forces with the Foundation.

OCTOBER 18. She inaugurates the new CGT headquarters, which she donated.

1951, FEBRUARY 20. The re-election of General Perón is proposed.

FEBRUARY 24. In a gathering of journalists commemorating the 1946 elections, a Perón-Evita ticket is called for.

APRIL 4. Eva reads excerpts from her official autobiography, *My Mission in Life*, before the visiting Prince Bernardo of Holland.

APRIL 9. She welcomes Golda Meier, then Israel's Minister of Public Works.

AUGUST 2. The Central Committee of the CGT publishes its resolution to vote for the Perón-Evita ticket in November.

AUGUST 22. A crowd forms in Cabildo Abierto, gathered by the CGT. Evita requests some time to decide whether or not she will join the ticket.

AUGUST 31. A radio message is broadcast in which she communicates her decision not to run.

SEPTEMBER 24. Advanced cancer prevents her from leaving the residence on Agüero and Libertador streets.

SEPTEMBER 28. Despite the fragile state of her health, Eva delivers a radio speech to her *descamisados* in response to General Menéndez's uprising.

OCTOBER 15. The book *My Mission in Life* is released.

OCTOBER 17. Eva delivers a dramatic speech and accepts the Perón Medal of Honor on the balcony of the *Casa Rosada*.

OCTOBER 27. She is too ill to attend the inauguration of the *Ciudad Estudiantil* (Students' Quarter).

NOVEMBER 6. Cancer specialist George Pack performs a hysterectomy

DECEMBER 24. In the Palacio Unzué (the residence), Evita gives away toys and chats with reporters.

1952, JANUARY 4. Evita attends an awards ceremony sponsored by the CGT.

JANUARY 10–11. She travels with Perón, but does not interact with the people.

MARCH 5. She attends the closing ceremonies of the Evita Children's Soccer Championship.

MARCH 28. She attends the Conference of Rural Workers and gives a speech about the Foundation's agrarian plan.

APRIL. She receives honors from the governments of Syria and Brazil. In spurts, she is dictating "My Message."

MAY 1. She attends the Workers' Celebration and delivers a violent speech condemning anti-Peronists.

MAY 7. Evita turns thirty-three.

JUNE 4. Against medical advice, she attends the swearing in of the re-elected Juan Perón. Her last public appearance is at Perón's side in the motorcade down the Avenida de Mayo.

JUNE 29. She signs her will, which is to be read aloud the next October 17.

JULY 20. An open-air mass is organized by the CGT.

JULY 26. At 10:25 PM, Evita dies in the residence on Agüero and Libertador streets.

ABOUT THE TRANSLATOR

Laura Dail's most recent translations include Cristina Peri Rossi's *Dostoevsky's Last Night* and Paco I. Taibo II's *Four Hands*. She holds a degree in linguistics from Duke University and a master's degree in Spanish literature from Middlebury College. She lives in New York City.